DRAMA AND READING FO AGES 4-11

Drama and Reading for Meaning Ages 4-11 contains over 40 creative drama ideas to help develop reading for meaning in the primary school. The wide range of clearly explained, structured and engaging drama activities will appeal to all primary practitioners who wish to develop more creative approaches to the teaching of reading. The activities show how drama can develop some of the skills associated with reading for meaning such as empathising with characters' feelings, exploring settings and themes and making inferences based on evidence.

The step-by-step activities range from familiar classroom drama strategies such as freeze-frames and hot-seating to less well-known approaches involving whole class drama experiences. The book also serves as an introduction to using drama as a learning medium, with advice on how to set the ground rules and clear explanations of the drama strategies. Each chapter has a detailed explanation of what to do, followed by a number of examples linked to quality texts, including poetry and non-fiction.

From bringing books to life in reception and Years 1 and 2, to peeling back the layers of meanings in Years 3 to 6, all the drama activities in this book are designed to improve reading for meaning and help motivate children to read for pleasure, making this an essential resource for all primary settings.

Larraine S. Harrison, formerly a local authority school improvement adviser and author of several drama books covering Early Years Foundation Stage (EYFS) to Key Stage 3, has spent many years promoting drama as a tool for teaching and learning. She is currently a part time drama-in-education consultant, school governor and author of two children's books: *Red Snow* and *Angel's Child*.

Do you want to develop children's imaginations and refresh your English teaching? Then look no further. This energising and accessible book will inspire teachers and children alike. Linked to literature and nonfiction texts, the step-by-step drama lessons support reading at greater depth and enable children to investigate characters' motivations, actions, and relationships, as well as explore real-life issues. A rich resource to support the development of language, interpretation and reading for meaning.

Teresa Cremin, Professor of Education (Literacy), The Open University, UK

DRAMA AND READING FOR MEANING AGES 4-11

A Practical Book of Ideas for Primary Teachers

Larraine S. Harrison

Routledge
Taylor & Francis Group
LONDON AND NEW YORK

Cover image: © Getty Images

First published 2022
by Routledge
4 Park Square, Milton Park, Abingdon, Oxon OX14 4RN

and by Routledge
605 Third Avenue, New York, NY 10158

Routledge is an imprint of the Taylor & Francis Group, an informa business

© 2022 Larraine S. Harrison

The right of Larraine S. Harrison to be identified as author of this work has been asserted in accordance with sections 77 and 78 of the Copyright, Designs and Patents Act 1988.

All rights reserved. No part of this book may be reprinted or reproduced or utilised in any form or by any electronic, mechanical, or other means, now known or hereafter invented, including photocopying and recording, or in any information storage or retrieval system, without permission in writing from the publishers.

Trademark notice: Product or corporate names may be trademarks or registered trademarks, and are used only for identification and explanation without intent to infringe.

British Library Cataloguing-in-Publication Data
A catalogue record for this book is available from the British Library

Library of Congress Cataloging-in-Publication Data
A catalog record for this book has been requested

ISBN: 978-1-032-16879-1 (hbk)
ISBN: 978-1-032-16880-7 (pbk)
ISBN: 978-1-003-25077-7 (ebk)

DOI: 10.4324/9781003250777

Typeset in Interstate
by Apex CoVantage, LLC

CONTENTS

Acknowledgements   viii

Introduction   1
What is this book about and who is it for?   1
Why use drama for reading?   1
How to manage drama   2
Frequently asked questions   6

PART I: AGES 4–6 (EYFS–YEAR 1)   9

1 **Collective re-enactment: ages 4–6**   11
   Performing rhymes and stories   12
   Celebrations   16
   Waving stick puppets   18
   Noisy books   20

2 **Characters and their problems**   29
   Letters from nursery rhyme characters   30
   Spontaneous role play   34
   Helping characters in stories   36
   Puppets with problems   38
   Helping imagined and minor characters   42
   Overheard conversations   46
   Role-on-the-wall   47

3 **Freezing key moments**   50
   A key moment   51
   Images   54
   Beginning, middle and end   55
   Predictions and alternatives   57
   Bringing frames to life   58
   Comparisons across texts   59

4 **An imaginary experience**   61
   A pet dragon   61
   Journey to topical places   64
   Caring for the environment   66

vi Contents

PART II: AGES 7-11 (YEARS 2-6)   73

5 Frozen depictions   75
   Exploring significant moments   76
   Recreating and creating images   81
   Freeze-frames in sequence   86
   The story of an object   88
   Read ... freeze ... read   90
   Predictions, alternatives and comparisons   92
   Information texts: depicting the main idea   93
   Group sculptures: capturing the essence   94

6 Actions and performances   97
   Action freeze narration   98
   The silent movie   100
   Actions for words and phrases   103
   Choral reading with actions   109
   Performing poems on a similar theme   110
   Performing riddles   111
   Improvisations   113
   On air   115
   Performing and presenting playscripts   118

7 Exploring characters   124
   Role-on-the-wall   125
   Variations on hot-seating   132
   The character circle   137
   Spotlighting/overheard conversations   141
   The line-up   144

8 Arguments, dilemmas and debates   146
   Arguments and opinions   146
   Dialogue for a dilemma   150
   Debates and trials   152

9 Settings, atmosphere and suspense   154
   Exploring a setting   155
   Sounds for words   159
   Characters as sounds   161
   A dreamy text   162
   Tracking the suspense   165

10 Whole group drama: the inside story   168
   An overview of whole group drama   169
   Dramatic play   170
   An extra scene   172
   Stepping into history   178
   Offering advice   185
   A similar story   187

Conclusion	194
The drama strategies	197
Further reading and resources	206
List of texts	208
Appendix: using live radio in schools	212

ACKNOWLEDGEMENTS

I would like to thank the many teachers, educators, authors, poets and playwrights who were kind enough to send me copies of books and offer their recommendations for accessible, quality children's texts. The wide range of texts I have been able to link with drama in this book reflects their contributions and is a testament to their generosity and knowledge of children's literature.

I would also like to give special thanks to the following people who have been a source of professional advice and support in the writing of this book: Teresa Cremin, Professor of Education at the Open University; Claire Davies, School Improvement Adviser for Reading, Waterton Multi-Academy Trust; Clare Putwain, Learnerama; and Jane Simpkins, School Improvement Adviser for Writing, Waterton Multi-Academy Trust.

In addition, I would like to thank the following people who generously offered me the benefit of their expertise and enthusiasm: Carol Allen, Margaret Branscombe, Pie Corbett, Vicki Murray and Routledge Education. Thanks also to Russell Prue for his advice on setting up and using radio in schools, some of which I have included as an appendix.

I am grateful to my son Kerry (www.kerryharrisonphotography.com) for his patience and technical support when preparing the illustrations and photographs for this book, and I would like to thank Sharlston Community School for the photograph of Rama and Sita.

I would also like to thank my husband Martyn for his continual advice, support and encouragement for this and my other writing projects over the past few years. Writing two children's novels, *Red Snow* and *Angel's Child*, has given me an additional perspective on authorial intent and emphasised the contribution authors can make to reading for meaning.

Finally, I would like to acknowledge the influence of the great pioneers in drama-in-education like Dorothy Heathcote, Gavin Bolton and Cecily O'Neill who first inspired me to use drama for teaching and learning and without whom this book would never have been written.

Introduction

What is this book about and who is it for?	1
Why use drama for reading?	1
How to manage drama	2
FAQs	6

What is this book about and who is it for?

This book is about how drama strategies can support the teaching of reading for meaning across the primary school. Designed as a bank of drama activities for primary teachers to integrate into their existing practice, it aims to raise awareness of the significant contribution drama can make to the teaching of reading. The cross-phase nature of the book also makes it a useful resource for English leaders, ITT tutors and other educators who seek to encourage a more creative approach to the teaching of reading.

The book includes guidance on how to manage the drama and how to make the experience more inclusive. The drama ideas range from simple classroom activities to whole class imaginary experiences. The activities are explained in detail for teachers with limited experience in drama, but more confident teachers can adapt them to their own ways of working. The numerous examples and further suggestions demonstrate how the drama strategies can support the exploration of a wide range of quality texts.

Many activities also include a section entitled 'Reader reflections' designed to facilitate the move from the particular text explored in the drama, to a broader more universal conversation about books and reading for pleasure. The drama strategies are made explicit within the activities, but are listed and defined at the end of the book for further clarification. The book concludes with comments from teachers and children, further reading and resources and a list of the texts for those who wish to source the books.

Why use drama for reading?

Drama-in-education is the shared experience of making meaning through the enactment of both real and fictional events. A shared exploration of a text through drama, where children make meaning together from *inside* the text, supports reading at greater depth and contributes to the development of a reading culture where children read for pleasure.

Drama can make a significant contribution to language and literacy, but when it's applied specifically to reading it enables children to explore the complexities of texts in an active, memorable and meaningful way. Stepping into an imaginary context encourages children to view texts through the lens of different perspectives, creating an opportunity to develop their interior visualisation, analysis and appreciation of all kinds of texts. It fosters an emotional engagement that can motivate and inspire children to peel back the layers of a text and dig a little deeper. In addition, each embodiment of and interaction with a text in drama creates a new representation of that text, which not only expands the meaning but supports greater recall.

Dramatic contexts create audience and purpose for reading. When imaginary situations create the need for children to engage in responsible, purposeful tasks, they become motivated to seek more information, ask questions, clarify, summarise, predict, make comparisons, solve problems, explore unfamiliar vocabulary and articulate what they know and understand. Drama experiences can therefore make a significant contribution towards reading comprehension, helping children become strategic readers of texts.

There are many occasions during drama where children are invited to formulate and express their opinions, but the opportunities for reflection following drama activities linked to texts, position children as readers with valued, informed opinions on those texts. It helps them understand that reading is a partnership between authorial intent and the reader's background knowledge, understanding and interpretation, thus challenging the perception of reading as a passive process: *'Reading comprehension is an active process of interactions between text and reader, which requires flexible integration of multiple strategies in order to construct meaning'* (Waterton Academy Trust. Delivering Excellence in Reading. Guidance Document. 2020).

Drama-in-education strategies work to enrich and deepen children's learning across the whole curriculum, but when they are integrated into the teaching of reading for meaning, drama becomes a form of reading in action with potential to make a significant contribution to reading at greater depth.

How to manage drama

The drama contract

Drama is unique in that it involves taking an active part in a fictional world, whilst at the same time being grounded in reality. Children taking part in drama straddle the line between fiction and reality, moving between the two worlds with relative ease. For drama to occur, children need to agree to behave as if they were somewhere else, somebody else or something else. This agreement to pretend is known as the drama contract. It may be informal or formal, explicit or implicit, but whatever form it takes, the drama contract is crucial to the success of the drama process. Confusion about expectations can undermine the drama process, leading to disengagement and frustration.

The way in which the contract is introduced will depend on the age and confidence of the children and the context of the drama. For very young children the contract may take the form of a more implicit exchange. For example: *'Excuse me Giants, can you show me how you walk with big steps?'*

By assuming the children are giants, the teacher is inviting the children to accept the pretence. If the children then respond by walking like giants, they are implicitly agreeing to accept that pretence.

However young children also understand when the contract is made more explicit. For example: *'When we start our drama, can you pretend you are giants walking with big steps?'* Older children respond best to a more explicit approach to the contract, using language more appropriate to their age group. For example: *'For this drama activity you need to take on the roles of/ play the parts of/imagine you are. . . . Will that be OK?'*

Drama is closely linked to stories and play and most children are keen to take part if the contract is presented in a positive way that assumes co-operation. Whilst all children should be encouraged to take part in a drama, there may be occasions when a child appears anxious or is reluctant to agree. This is more likely to occur if they are new to drama work. The way you respond depends on your knowledge of the child, but an invitation to observe until the child feels more comfortable or able to accept the pretence is often all that is required. When children see others enjoying the drama, they usually opt to accept the contract and join in.

Defining the space

It's important to define the drama space before you begin so that children are clear about any areas and items that are out of bounds.

Stopping and starting

Use clear signals for stopping and starting the drama, such as the words 'action' and 'freeze'. You can use different sounds instead of these words, but whatever you choose needs to be used consistently, so you can manage the drama process at all times.

Time to think

Children cannot produce their best work if they are given insufficient time to think and prepare for a task and this also applies to drama. Clear step-by-step instructions with time to think in between, are key to the successful management of a drama lesson and are particularly important for children who prefer to make thoughtful, considered responses. However, there may be occasions when a more spontaneous response is required. Whether you give children notice of this beforehand will depend on your knowledge of the children.

Choosing the best drama strategy

Your choice of strategy is an important factor in the successful management of the drama. The choice will depend on a number of considerations including the specific needs of the children, the learning objectives and the themes covered in the texts. Drama strategies offering a degree of distancing for example, may be more appropriate for dealing with sensitive themes. Re-enactments, improvisations and even freeze-frames depicting sensitive situations in texts can be too close to reality for some children and difficult for them to portray without embarrassment or distress. Other strategies such as interviewing a teacher-in-role or hot-seating characters may be more appropriate as they allow children to consider the impact of those issues on an imaginary third party. Role-on-the-wall is another strategy that allows children to explore sensitive issues at a distance. If the issue is one that may prove difficult for a particular child, it may be worth talking to them beforehand to explain what to expect in the drama and allow you to respond to any concerns they may have.

Another important consideration in the choice of strategy is your own level of confidence and experience in drama and your teaching style. Every teacher is different, so if you are new to drama it's best to start with the drama strategies you feel comfortable with. That way you can build up your repertoire from a confident base.

Teacher-in-role

Teacher-in-role is a powerful drama strategy with enormous potential for teaching and learning, but one which teachers often find challenging. Setting it up clearly and carrying it out with integrity are the keys to avoiding pitfalls and maximising its effectiveness. If you are joining the children as one of the group in the drama, you can assume that role with little need for explanation. However, if you are adopting a more specific role, it's important to ensure the children will accept you in that role before you begin. This may be just a simple request but its function is similar to that of the drama contract. Putting on a small item of clothing or holding an object as a sign of teacher-in-role will make it clear for everyone and enable you to move in and out of role during the drama whenever you need to. If children become confused at any point, you can pause the drama, remove the sign of role and remind them of their agreement to accept you in that role. It's rare for a child to have a problem with agreeing to a teacher-in-role, but if it should happen, invite that child to observe whilst you are in role. Most children appreciate the fact that a teacher is willing to take on a role and if you assume co-operation and introduce the role with confidence, most children will be keen to agree.

It's not necessary to have great acting skills to use teacher-in-role. In fact, over-acting or putting on a vastly different voice can be distracting. The key to success is performing the role with integrity. If you are new to using teacher-in-role, try telling a story as if you were one of the minor characters or take on an authority or leadership role within the drama context such as a mayor, monarch or community leader.

Roles have different statuses within the drama, ranging from a high-status role of someone in authority, through to an equal status role as one of the group, to a low status role of a needy person seeking help. If you are new to teacher-in-role you may want to start with a high-status role, but equal and lower status roles are more effective in facilitating talk and independent learning. Teachers who are confident with this strategy can play more than one role in a drama, varying the status of the roles according to need.

The choice of role depends not only on your own confidence, but on the function you want the role to play. Whatever role you play, you will always be the teacher with a focus on the learning. Be clear about what you want the role to achieve e.g. will it provide information, pose a problem, make a request for information or deepen the thinking? If you have a particular character you want to focus on, it may be better to play a role connected to that character rather than the character themselves. This means you don't have to mimic the person or know everything about them. However, the role you choose does need to know the character well or have some information about them e.g. a close relative, friend, fellow pupil or colleague, housekeeper, cleaner, servant, messenger, neighbour, bystander, researcher or a journalist who has written an article about the character. Each role offers a different perspective. If you set up teacher-in-role with clarity and carry it out with integrity, you can adopt any role you choose. Even animal or creature roles are possible if you explain to the children beforehand that you will not try to sound or look like the animal you are playing.

Inclusion

Whilst most children are able and willing to take part in drama activities, there may be times when adaptations are needed to ensure all children are given an opportunity to participate. Inclusive practices across the curriculum apply equally to drama work. Practices such as clear explanations and instructions, suitably paced challenges, plenty of time for children to think, plan and respond and pre-teaching key vocabulary with pictures and symbols are all relevant to drama activities. Other adaptations for drama may include practical adjustments like making sure the space is adequate for all children to take part and making sure all children have suitable access to the texts if and when required.

If the children are new to drama, some may need more time to adjust. Children who find imagining and pretending difficult may struggle with the idea of taking on a role because it is not *real*. Choosing drama contexts based on real life events, along with simple explanations of how the drama links to the objective, e.g. '*This will help us understand . . . learn more about . . . show how . . . etc.*' can sometimes alleviate their concerns. Cautious children can also be offered an observational role such as an artist, note-taking journalist or documentary-maker recording the drama on video. Younger children often like to take on jobs such as the keeper of the props, the time-keeper or the teacher's helper.

There are other occasions when the opposite occurs. A child will take on a role with such enthusiasm that they want to continue to play that same role in subsequent dramas, no matter what the context. This can be challenging but can sometimes be accommodated by suggesting the role has different characteristics or performs different tasks each time. If this situation occurs, be as flexible and patient as you can and try not to draw attention to it. This helps the child to move on and helps reduce the potential for others to become distracted.

Some children find it difficult to come out of role after the drama has finished. Time to wind down after the drama along with activities such as waving an imaginary wand to make the character disappear or pretending to take off an invisible character costume can help younger children. Older children often benefit from advanced warning and plenty of time to reflect out of role.

Whether children are cautious or enthusiastic, helping them to understand the nature of drama, what it helps them learn and what it means to take part is crucial. For some children this may take time, so as with any other learning area, patience, understanding and appropriate support are key.

Drama-in-education is by nature an inclusive practice and many children with special and additional needs blossom and excel within a dramatic context, leading to improvements in their self-esteem and increased self-confidence within their group.

Frequently asked questions

How can I use drama with quiet or shy children who are reluctant to perform?

Whilst drama-in-education can include plays and improvisations, it is not primarily about theatre skills. The focus of drama-in-education is on enactment rather than performance. It seeks to place children in imaginary contexts which require them to respond as if those contexts were real. However, the degree to which they respond is a matter of choice and not dictated. Whilst all children should be given the opportunity and support to build their confidence through performing for an audience, there should always be an equally acceptable alternative choice for those who do not choose to perform. No child should be made to feel inadequate because they do not wish to perform in front of an audience. Teachers need to use their knowledge of each child to make a decision as to whether a cautious child would benefit from being encouraged to perform or not. Sometimes it is just a case of explaining the reason for the performance in terms of learning or allowing sufficient time for children to consider and prepare. However, many drama strategies do not involve any kind of performance. Choose the drama strategies that suit your learning objectives, but be prepared to adapt them with sensitivity to accommodate the various needs of the children.

Do we need a large space for drama?

The short answer is no. Many drama strategies can take place in the classroom, without the need to move the furniture. There are some that undoubtedly work best in a cleared or larger space, but if necessary these can be adapted to the classroom environment. Where a drama involves a sequence of lessons it's often useful to use a larger space for at least one of the lessons.

How do I keep control of a lively class during a drama lesson?

Drama-in-education is a very structured approach to learning. Whilst it gives children a certain amount of freedom, it also requires the setting of clear boundaries and expectations. Start with the contract, define the space and be consistent with your expectations. Most children are keen to abide by the rules if the reasons for them are explained. A quiet word with individual children who fail to follow the rules is often all that is required. If there are problems with several children, stop the drama immediately, explain the problem and renegotiate. Be prepared to do this as many times as it takes, until they become used to the expectations. This may be tough at first but children are usually keen to take part in drama and most will be prepared to respect the ground rules if they are explained clearly and applied consistently.

Choose a drama strategy that both you and the children will be comfortable with. If drama is a new experience for everyone, start with a structured activity like a whole class freeze-frame, moving on to more ambitious approaches like whole group drama when you feel more confident.

Making your drama sufficiently engaging is also important when teaching a lively group, but every class is different and if you feel the drama isn't engaging the children, be prepared to stop. Try to find out what went wrong, either from the children and/or from reflecting on the lesson afterwards. Ask yourself if there was anything you could have done to engage the children more effectively before trying again. Not all drama strategies suit the needs of every group at any one time, so start with the strategy you feel is most likely to succeed and build on that success.

How can I fit drama into an already crowded curriculum?

Where drama is used as a teaching tool, as in this book, it becomes a means to an end, rather than a discreet subject requiring extra time. The drama strategies themselves also vary in the time they take to complete. If time is a problem, start with one of the shorter activities and build up your repertoire, so drama becomes an integral part of your teaching toolkit. You will find the impact is well worth the time invested.

I'm not good at acting and don't enjoy drama, so how can I use it to teach?

Drama as a teaching method is not about theatre. It does not require great acting skills and does not necessarily have to involve performance. Look at the list of drama strategies in this book and select those you feel comfortable with. For example, teacher-in-role is an excellent strategy to work towards but you can achieve a similar outcome via an imaginary letter or message from a character. The important thing is that all the adults involved in the drama approach it in a positive manner, taking on any roles with integrity so they model and present drama to the children as a legitimate way of learning. Drama is such a powerful teaching tool, but like any other area of learning, it needs to be adapted to your own situation and the needs of the children.

Do children need to warm up with a drama game before taking part in drama?

Drama games are designed to develop children's personal, emotional and social skills and can make a valuable contribution to learning. They are often used by high school drama teachers as warm ups for improvisation work or theatre. However, in primary schools, unless they make a significant contribution to the theme of the drama, they are best carried out in a separate lesson. It is rarely practical to use warm ups where drama forms an integral part of a reading lesson and it can be challenging to introduce a drama about a serious issue after a lively game. If the drama is introduced in a structured way where children are given time to think and prepare, there is less need for a warm up.

Can you use drama strategies with guided reading groups?

Guided reading usually takes place in a classroom alongside other children who may be distracted by physically active or vocal drama work. However, less physically active strategies such as role-on-the-wall, hot-seating, teacher-in-role and mantle-of-the-expert can work well in a guided reading group. Groups can also research texts for future whole class drama work such as identifying key moments for freeze-frames, suggesting questions for hot-seating or reading texts in preparation to be hot-seated as a group representing a character or creatures. Some books such as my *Angel's Child*, for example, include guided reading questions for every chapter with suggested responses. These can form the basis for exploring key moments to create Thought Bubbles and captions for future freeze-frames or in preparation for being hot-seated by the rest of the class. The drama thus provides an audience and purpose for guided reading work.

Do I need a collection of props and costumes to use drama?

A large collection of props and costumes is not necessary for drama-in-education work. It is possible to use all the drama strategies in this book with just a scarf, a puppet and some cardboard signs. Too many props can be distracting. However, some extra items can be useful. Masks are an option for representing some characters, but children often benefit from making their own. These can be simple paper face masks or those made of stiff card held in front of the face like paddles. Alternatively, you can purchase ready-made masks of characters in well-known stories such as The Three Little Pigs and other fairy tales.

A length of luxurious cloth and a length of rough cloth are also useful to drape over chairs to depict thrones or poorer settings and can be used as cloaks for teacher-in-role. Any other items relating to particular stories can usually be accessed from school or home, so whilst it may be a good idea to collect the equivalent of a small capsule wardrobe for drama, there is no need to accumulate a vast number of costumes or props.

Can drama be adapted for distance learning?

Drama is a social activity and face to face experience is the best way to engage in drama. However, if face to face teaching is not possible for any reason, some drama strategies can be adapted for online lessons. Some activities in this book include a section on adapting drama for distance learning.

PART I

Ages 4-6 (EYFS-Year 1)

Figure I.1 Singing on the bus

These structured drama activities for 4-6-year-olds are designed to form part of a wide range of language and literacy experiences that develop children's understanding of texts. They seek to complement a language-rich environment where children have access to a wide range of stories, rhymes and other texts. Whilst the suggested activities work best with children ages 4 to 6 (EYFS-Year 1) in mainstream schools, they should always be adapted to the needs of the children and the context of the school or setting.

The duration of each activity depends on the children's responses, but most are designed to last no longer than twenty or thirty minutes.

Ages 4-6 (EYFS-Year 1)

The nursery rhymes and traditional tales referred to in Part I are linked to the following texts:

Usborne Illustrated Book of Nursery Rhymes chosen by Felicity Brooks
Mother Goose's Nursery Rhymes by Axel Scheffler
Ladybird Tales: Classic Collection by Ladybird
Usborne Illustrated Fairy Tales by Rosie Dickins

1 Collective re-enactment
Ages 4-6

LINKS TO READING FOR MEANING: engaging with texts; dramatising stories; empathy; inference; recall; sequencing; exploring mood and settings; identifying direct speech; reading for a purpose; comparing texts; identifying favourite parts of stories.

Rationale

Physical involvement in rhymes and stories helps children engage with texts and develops the skills of recall and sequencing. Taking part in a whole school performance based on a well-known story such as *The Gruffalo Play* by Julia Donaldson can be a valuable and memorable experience for children, but the amount of preparation required often limits the frequency of such an opportunity.

Inviting a small group of children to re-enact a rhyme or story for the rest of the group is more achievable on a regular basis and can help both the performers and audience understand, picture and sequence the events. However, whilst this is a valuable experience, collective re-enactment offers all children an opportunity to re-enact the events simultaneously without an audience. This makes it an ideal activity for children who are reluctant to perform in front of others. Listening to a story in order to re-enact it can also be an incentive to pay more attention to the meaning.

Contents

Performing rhymes and stories	12
Celebrations	16
Waving stick puppets	18
Noisy books: Poems, Stories and Settings	20

Drama strategies

Actions
Action freeze narration
Freeze

DOI: 10.4324/9781003250777-3

Ages 4-6 (EYFS-Year 1)

Puppets on sticks
Sound effects
Soundscapes
Teacher-in-role

Performing rhymes and stories

Performing nursery rhymes

This is a short activity where the children move as if they were a character from a well-known nursery rhyme and freeze in role when the teacher calls the word *'freeze.'* The act of freezing the moment slows down the action so the teacher can focus the children's attention on the characters and their feelings.

Planning and resources

- Select a character from a familiar rhyme with potential for movement and mime e.g. Jack or Jill walking up the hill; Goosey Gander or Wee Willie Winkie climbing stairs; the Grand Old Duke of York marching etc.

You will need:

- A space with room for children to move around.
- Image(s) depicting your chosen character.

What to do

- Ask the children to walk around the room without touching anyone else. They should move when you say the word *'go'* and stop in a frozen position when you say *'freeze.'* Then unfreeze them with an imaginary invisible magic wand.
- Repeat until most children are able to follow these instructions.
- Display the image(s) of the character and ask them to guess the rhyme.
- Ask the children to demonstrate how they might move if they were this character at a given point in the rhyme, e.g. *'How can we move like we are Jack or Jill climbing the steep hill? . . . climbing stairs like Wee Willy Winkie?'* Add your own suggestions if necessary but try to use as many of the children's ideas as possible.

Version 1

- On the word *'go,'* invite the children to move as if they were that character until you stop them with *'freeze.'*

Version 2

- Create a follow-the-leader type of activity, where children copy you as you lead them around the room, moving as if you were the character according to the children's suggestions. Stop on the word *'freeze'* each time.

Both versions

- Ask the children to hold the freeze until you unfreeze them with your magic wand.
- Comment briefly but positively on children's frozen depictions of the character before you unfreeze everyone.
- Bring the children together and talk about how that character might be feeling. Use this as an opportunity to extend vocabulary and encourage empathy, e.g. Jack and Jill may be feeling tired, Wee Willie Winkie is worried, the Grand Old Duke of York's soldiers may be bored, etc. Talk about how the character's feelings might affect how they move.
- Repeat the activity with the suggested adaptations to incorporate the character's feelings.
- Conclude by inviting the children to recite the rhyme along with you.
- If appropriate you can repeat the whole activity with another character from a different rhyme. You may want to invite a child to be the leader in the second version.

Extension activity

Children draw pictures of themselves as the character they played. Use this as an opportunity to remind the children how their character was feeling.

Further Suggestions

Select people, animals or creatures linked to topic books for the activity e.g. children move as if they are jungle creatures, astronauts, mini beasts, undersea creatures etc.

Performing Stories

The previously described nursery rhyme activity can be extended to re-enact short stories or parts of longer stories. The stories can be divided into short sections according to their potential for actions. The word 'go' can also be replaced by the more drama related word 'action.'

Use Example 1 as a model for re-enacting other stories:

EXAMPLE 1: LITTLE BOY KRISHNA AND THE BUTTER

Text: *Stories from Faiths:* **Hinduism. Krishna steals the butter and other stories by Anita Ganeri**

Planning and resources

Divide the events in the story into short sections according to opportunities for children to mime Krishna's actions. They can change role to play the part of his mother for the last section if you wish. Plan to tell each section in your own words, but keep it simple so children can identify the actions, e.g. *'Krishna drank some milk from one of the buckets and dipped his fingers into the butter. It tasted so good.'* Mimes for this section could be drinking the milk, dipping a finger into butter, smiling or licking his lips as he enjoys the taste.

You will need:

- Space with room for children to move around.
- A copy of the story to read to the children.
- A small selection of story books with characters who do naughty things like Krishna in this story.

What to do

- Read and/or tell the story to the children before the drama, introducing any background information, new vocabulary and ideas as and when appropriate.
- Invite the children to join you in acting out the story.
- Narrate your prepared sections of the story, asking the children what happens next and how the character might be feeling at this point, before discussing potential mimed actions for the forthcoming section. Give children the opportunity to suggest and/or demonstrate their own ideas before adding your own.
- Perform the story using the words '*action*' and '*freeze*' to start and stop each section.
- After the first run through, repeat again without the intervening discussion, so the sequence flows.
- Mention the way the characters were feeling in different parts of the story and ask the children to share their favourite parts.

Reader reflections

Ask:

- *'Do you enjoy stories about characters who do naughty things like Krishna?'*
- *'Have we read any other stories with characters who do naughty things?'*

　　　Refer to some of the stories you have read with the children that might fit these criteria, e.g. **Where the Wild Things Are by Maurice Sendak**, and use them to prompt further discussion.

Extension activity

Children recall and draw their favourite part of the Krishna and the butter story.

EXAMPLE 2: *MEG AND MOG* BY HELEN NICOLL AND JAN PIENKOWSKI

Proceed as in Example 1 with the following adaptations:

Planning and resources

You will need:

- Other books about witches, including any the children have read before.

What to do

This story is full of simple actions that can be organised into sections as in Example 1 and mimed in a similar way. Read the story to the children beforehand, asking them to listen carefully and look at the pictures so they can act it out later.

> **Reader reflections**
>
> Ask:
>
> - 'Have we read any other stories about witches?'
> - 'I wonder if the witches in other stories dress like Meg and do similar things. Let's look at the books to find out.'
> - 'Do you know why witches have a broomstick and a cauldron?'
>
>   Link to books like **Room on the Broom** by **Julia Donaldson** and explore the similarities and differences.

EXAMPLE 3: LITTLE RED RIDING HOOD

Texts:

- **Little Red Riding Hood:** a traditional version
- (Optional) *Red Riding Hood and the Sweet Little Wolf* by Rachael Mortimer

Planning, resources and what to do

Proceed as in Example 1 with the following adaptations:

Ages 4–6 (EYFS–Year 1)

The traditional version:

- Longer stories like this can be divided into more sections where the children play a different role in each section:

  1. The children play the part of Little Red Riding Hood
  2. The children play the part of the wolf
  3. The children play the part of the woodcutter

- You may want to focus on just one section when working with the youngest children.
- Read the part of the story you will focus on before the activity, asking children to play close attention so they can act it out later.
- After the drama ask children how they felt when playing the characters. If they acted out more than one section, ask them which character they preferred to play.
- Conclude by re-reading or revising the traditional story.

An alternative version

- Read **Red Riding Hood and the Sweet Little Wolf by Rachel Mortimer.**
- Use collective re-enactment to act out different parts of this story as previously described. Then talk about the similarities and differences between this and the traditional version.

Further Suggestions

Funnybones by Janet and Allan Ahlberg

Use collective re-enactment to act out the activities of the skeletons at the beginning of this story.

Celebrations

Many traditional and other stories involve large group events such as celebrations, offering opportunities for children to take part in an imaginary version. Joining in with part of a story in this way helps bring the story to life for the children. Use the following example as a model for other stories:

EXAMPLE: SLEEPING BEAUTY'S CHRISTENING PARTY

Planning and resources

- This activity works best with a smaller group

You will need:

- A copy of the story.
- Resources for children to make simple gifts for the baby princess.

Collective re-enactment

- Space for children to sit in a large semicircle.
- An item of clothing to represent the king or queen, e.g. a crown or rich fabric for a cloak.
- An invitation for the children to attend the christening party with the good fairies.
- A doll in a crib, suitably dressed to represent the baby princess.
- A letter to the children from the palace, thanking them for their gifts.

What to do

Preparation

- Read the beginning of the story to the children where the good fairies are invited to attend the christening party. Ask the children to pretend they have been invited to this event along with the good fairies and read them the invitation from the king and queen.
- Talk about and share experiences of what happens at this kind of event and how they will need to make gifts for the baby before they go to the christening party.
- Invite the children to make the gifts. Talk about what a baby would like and what kind of gifts can be made with the resources available. Some children may like to work in pairs to make a gift. Talk to the children as they make their gifts and ask them about their choices.

The drama

- Arrange the children in a semicircle facing the cot. Ask the children to pretend this is a room in the palace where the christening party will take place and the doll in the cot is the baby princess.
- Ask them to pretend you will be the king or queen when wearing the cloak or crown.
- Introduce the words '*action*' and '*freeze*' to start and stop the drama.
- Use simple but formal, regal language in role as the king or queen. Thank the guests and explain that the princess is asleep. Invite them to take turns to place their gifts quietly by the cot. Ask each guest or pair of guests to state what gift they have brought and ask them a question about it.
- Children must leave the party quietly as the princess is still asleep.
- Stop the drama with the word '*freeze*' and take off the cloak or crown to come out of role. Make it clear that their story has finished.
- Ask the children what parts they liked best and how they felt.
- Re-read the part of the story involving the christening party and talk about what happened next in the story. Talk about why the bad fairy was angry and what she did as a result.
- After the drama, send the children a thank you letter from the palace.

Further Suggestions

- Children are invited to Cinderella or Snow White's wedding party.
- **Meg on the Moon by Helen Nicoll and Jan Pienkowski:** Children make and send cards for Mog's third birthday and receive a thank you letter from Meg, telling the children how they all went to the moon for Mog's birthday treat.

- **The Very Hungry Caterpillar's Birthday Party by Eric Carle:** Children make birthday cards to send to the caterpillar and receive a thank you note telling them all about the party.

Waving stick puppets

Simple stick puppets made by the children, provide them with an opportunity to contribute to a story or a poem in an interactive and meaningful way. Anticipating when and how to join in helps children develop the skills of recall, retelling and sequencing and helps them identify direct speech.

Children make stick puppets of characters or objects in a story or poem and wave them during the reading, whenever their character speaks or their object is mentioned. The activity works best using texts with repeated words or phrases.

Use the following examples as models for other stories:

EXAMPLE 1: THE GINGERBREAD MAN

This example involves all children waving their puppets and saying the same words at the same time.

Planning and resources

You will need:

- A copy of the story to read aloud during the activity.
- Resources for every child to make a simple stick puppet of the Gingerbread Man before the activity.

What to do

- Read the story to the children, asking them to listen out for when the Gingerbread Man speaks, so they know when to wave their puppets.
- Read again, inviting the children to wave their stick puppets carefully in the air whenever the Gingerbread Man says *'Run, run as fast as you can. You can't catch me, I'm the Gingerbread Man.'* Children can join in with these words but should put their puppets down when the Gingerbread Man is not speaking.
- Talk about how the Gingerbread man was feeling when he spoke these words and what his voice might sound like if he was feeling this way.
- Encourage the children to say the words as if they really were the Gingerbread Man.

EXAMPLE 2: THE LITTLE RED HEN

This is a more sophisticated version of waving puppets, requiring more anticipation and listening for meaning.

What to do

Proceed as in Example 1 with the following adaptations:

- Groups of children make different stick puppets for the characters who talk to the Red Hen, e.g. one group makes dog puppets, the other cat puppets, etc. Make sure every child has a puppet and knows which group they are in.
- Children need to sit with their group and their puppet as they listen to the story.
- Read the story, asking the different groups to wave their puppets and join in with the words when their character is speaking.
- Ask the children how they might make the characters' voices sound different to show which character is speaking. Ask how each character is feeling when they say their words and how this might affect the way they speak. Then repeat the activity.

EXAMPLE 3: *THE BIG BAD MOLE'S COMING* BY MARTIN WADDELL AND JOHN BENDALL-BRUNELLO

This is an excellent book to perform with stick puppets and provides a good introduction to speech bubbles. It also helps develop inferential understanding when the animals suddenly change their predictable sounds.

The level of challenge in this version of waving puppets makes it particularly suitable for Year 1. Children need to see the speech bubbles clearly in the book, which may make this activity more suited to a smaller group.

What to do

Proceed as in Example 1 with the following adaptations:

- Groups make stick puppets of the main animal characters.
- Children wave their puppets and make the appropriate animal sounds when you point to the speech bubbles for their animal. Draw their attention to any clues in the text about the changes in volume. Warn them to be ready to change their sounds when they come to one particular key moment.
- Talk about what made the animals suddenly change their sounds at this point and why they then went back to normal again.

EXAMPLE 4: *ODD SOCKS* BY NEAL ZETTER

This book is a poem about what happened to a variety of odd socks. The repetition and predictable text in relation to how different socks disappeared, makes it an ideal performance poem for stick puppets of sock outlines, coloured according to those in the poem.

Ages 4-6 (EYFS-Year 1)

What to do

Proceed as in Example 1 with the following adaptations:

- Children wave their puppet when their particular sock is mentioned during the reading.
- Read a second time with the puppets, but this time ask all children to join in by chanting the question that precedes the appearance of each sock. Confident children may also like to join in with other repetitive phrases such as the first and last lines of the book.
- Draw attention to the question mark on every page and use this as an opportunity to talk about the function of this punctuation mark in a text.
- Ask children to stand up, make a curved shape with their hands above their heads to make the shape of a question mark and do a little jump for the dot.

> ### Reader reflections
>
> Ask: 'Have we read any other stories or poems about clothes?'
>
> Link to books such as **Socks by Nick Sharratt and Elizabeth Lindsay** and ***Aliens Love Underpants* by Claire Freedman.**
> Show children another text with question marks and ask them to help you spot them as you turn the pages.

Further Suggestions

The Highway Rat by Julia Donaldson

Children make stick puppets of the Highway Rat to wave and chant when they hear the repetitive phrase from the rat. Ask the children how the rat was feeling as he was speaking these words and ask them to suggest ways to show this in their voices.

Noisy books

Linking the words in texts to different sounds and actions, requires children to engage with the meanings of those words, making this a useful activity in the development of reading for meaning.

1   *Noisy poems*

Planning and resources

- Select a short poem that suggests different sounds or voices such as:

***The Sound Collector* by Roger McGough**
***Ears Hear* by Lucia and James L Hymes Jnr**
***On the Nong Nang Ning* by Spike Milligan**

(All three can be found in *Noisy Poems* by Debi Gliori.)
Voices of Water **by Tony Mitton** from ***Poems to Perform*** **by Julia Donaldson**

You will need:

- Suitable percussion instruments and other objects which can be used to represent some of the sounds in the chosen poem.

What to do

- Display the instruments and objects where the children can see them.
- Read the poem to the children, asking them to listen for any opportunities for making sounds as you read.
- Identify where different sounds could be made in the poem.
- Ask the children for suggestions and demonstrations on how they could make these different sounds by using their voices, objects or instruments. Consider each sound in turn.
- Allocate different sounds to pairs or groups of children, making sure everyone is responsible for at least one sound.
- Make an agreement that no-one makes their sound unless it is their turn in the poem.
- Add actions if appropriate.
- Read the poem again, pausing to allow the children to make the appropriate sounds at the appropriate times.
- Repeat to develop confidence in anticipating when to make the sounds.

Reader reflections

Ask:

- 'Did you enjoy adding extra sounds to a poem?'
- 'Do you like listening to a poem with extra sounds or would you rather listen without the sounds? Why do you think that?'

Extension activity

Present the poem as a performance to another adult or group of children and/or make an audio recording for the children to reflect on and identify the sounds they made.

2 Noisy stories

Children can create different sounds or use different voices to represent all or part of a story during a reading. The need to know what sounds are appropriate and when to make them, helps children understand the sequence of events and consider the meaning.

Ages 4-6 (EYFS-Year 1)

Version 1: voices

Planning and resources

- Select a story where the characters say simple words or sounds, preferably using different kinds of voices or speak at different volumes.
- All children need sight of this text during the activity.

What to do

- Read the story to the children, asking them to notice when and how the characters use their voices.
- Invite the children to make the sounds or say the words spoken by the characters during the next reading. Use this as an opportunity to talk about how the characters are feeling and/or why they are making the sounds or saying the words in this way etc. If appropriate to the text, warn them to watch out for any clues in the reading such as large type and/or bold print to indicate the volume.
- Go through the story to locate, identify and practise the sounds.
- Practise reading with the added voices before a final performance, which can be recorded for children to listen to later. A recorded version provides an opportunity for children to evaluate how effective their version was in relation to the meaning of the story.

EXAMPLE: SHHH! QUIET BY NICOLA KINNEAR

Proceed as in Version 1 with the following adaptations:

- Talk about the different sizes of text when the animals make noises and what that means in terms of volume and feelings.
- Invite the children to voice the words in large print when you next read the story. Go through the book asking the children to help you spot any words in larger print and talk about why there is a difference in size. Then practise how each of the words might be voiced to reflect the intended volume and associated feelings.
- Finally read the book as the children voice the appropriate sounds.

Reader reflections

Invite discussion on the theme of the story by reflecting on questions such as:

'I wonder if it's ever OK to be noisy.'
'Is there a good time to be quiet?'

> 'Are some people quieter than others?'
> 'Can people get upset if others are very quiet? Or if they are very noisy?'
> 'I didn't like it when those characters shouted all the time. I felt sorry for little fox. How did you feel?'
> 'I wonder if it's important to listen to people. Was it important in this story?'

Version 2: sound effects

Planning and resources

- All the children need sight of a copy of the chosen story.
- Decide on a suitable signal to start and/or stop the sound effects.
- Select places in the text where you can pause for sound effects.

You will need:

- Percussion instruments suited to the sounds in the story; one for each child.

What to do

- Arrange the instruments in groups according to the type of sounds they make and sit with the children in a circle or semicircle.
- Demonstrate or remind the children how each of the instruments should be used.
- Keeping the instruments in their groups, place an instrument in front of each child, asking them not to touch the instruments until you give the signal.
- When you raise your hand the children should play their instruments but when you give the agreed signal (e.g. blow a whistle or clap), they should stop and put the instruments down.
- Practise this until the children are confident at following the instructions.
- Ask the children to help you find places in the chosen story where they can use the instruments to make sound effects. Read up to the first opportunity for a sound effect. Explain that you will pause here during the reading, so children can make the sounds.
- Talk about what instruments might make the best sounds for this section of the story and how they need to be played to make these sounds e.g. quietly, loudly, quickly etc.
- Read this part of the story again and pause at the first sound effect. Then raise your hand as a signal for the children to respond with sounds.
- Stop the activity using the agreed signal.
- When children are confident with this first section, repeat with the rest of the story if appropriate.

> **Reader reflections**
>
> Ask:
>
> - 'Do you like listening to a story with sound effects or is it better without them and why?'
> - 'Has anyone watched stories on video or TV with sound effects? What kind of sound effects were they? How did they make you feel?'

> **Extension activities**
>
> Perform for another adult or another group of children.
> When children are confident with using sound effects, involve them in deciding which instruments might be appropriate for other stories.

EXAMPLE 1: *WHERE THE WILD THINGS* ARE BY MAURICE SENDAK

Proceed as in Version 2 with the following adaptations:

What to do

- Read the story to the children, asking them to notice if any creatures make sounds.
- Work as a class to create the sounds of the Wild Things.
- Children should perform the sounds whenever the Wild Things appear in the story.
- Ask if they should use different sounds for when Max returns to his bedroom. They could try to make quieter sounds to accompany that part of the story.
- Practise and then do a final performance.

> **Extension activity**
>
> Create a dance with the sounds, to reflect the Rumpus.

EXAMPLE 2: THE THREE LITTLE PIGS WITH ACTIONS

Proceed as in Version 2 but with the following adaptations:

Planning and resources

You will need:

- A copy of the *Three Little Pigs*.
- (Optional) A whistle or other loud instrument as a signal to stop.
- Percussion instruments, one for each child, to cover the following three groups:

    a   Light sounds, e.g. tambourine, rain-stick, cabasa, wind chimes and triangle.
    b   Wooden sounds, e.g. woodblock, wooden agogo, castanets, claves, guiro.
    c   Harsh sounds, e.g. cymbal, cowbell, tambour, snare drum, bongos.

What to do

- Sit with the children in a circle or semicircle and display the instruments. Explain that these instruments will help tell the story of *The Three Little Pigs*.
- Keeping the instruments in their groups, place one in front of each child, but ask them not to touch them until you give a signal.
- Read the story up to the point where the first pig builds a house of straw. Then stop to ask which group of instruments they could use to sound like the pig is building a straw house.
- Allow the children with the lighter sounding instruments to practise playing them to represent building the house with straw. Suggest accompanying mimed actions for the rest of the group, such as cutting straw, twisting straw into bundles and building the walls of straw house.
- Proceed in the same way for building the wooden house with the wooden sounding instruments. Actions could be sawing wood, hammering nails and putting in screws.
- Continue in same way for building the brick house with the harsh sounding instruments. Actions could be mixing cement and laying bricks with a trowel.
- Finish with all the children playing their instruments as the wolf falls down the chimney.
- Read or tell the story, pausing to allow the children to play and perform their actions at the appropriate points.

Reader reflections

Ask:

- 'Which part of the story did you like the best and why?'
- 'How did it make you feel when we all made the sounds as the wolf fell down the chimney?'

EXAMPLE 3: THE THREE BILLY GOATS GRUFF

This activity offers more challenge, as some of the required sounds are more abstract and children are asked to select the appropriate instruments.

Planning, resources and what to do

- Proceed in the same way as The Three Little Pigs example, but without grouping the instruments.
- Use the following sections for sound effects:

  a   Goats skipping on the grass at the start and end.
  b   Goats trip trapping over the bridge.
  c   Scary sounds for the troll.

- Place a range of instruments in front of the children and ask them to decide which are the most appropriate for each section and what actions can be used.
- Perform as in the *Three Little Pigs* example.

Further Suggestions

Rabunzel *by Gareth P. Jones*

The sounds of the hungry eyed creatures can be created and performed during the reading, along with chanting the repeated phrase. Compare this story to the story of Rapunzel.

All Are Welcome Here *by Alexandra Penfold*

Children decide on appropriate background sounds and an action to depict the idea of a *welcome*. Allocate a group to make the sounds as the rest perform the action, when repeating the phrase '*All are welcome here*' during the reading. Talk about how children might feel when they hear that phrase spoken in their school.

3   Noisy settings

This activity involves producing a soundscape stimulated by the setting of a book.

Planning and resources

- Select a story with a setting that involves, or has potential to involve sounds.
- Children need access to the description of the setting in the chosen story.

You will need:

- Percussion instruments to make the appropriate sounds.

What to do

- Using the book as a prompt, talk about what sounds you might hear in the setting.
- Help the children decide which instruments to use to make these kinds of sounds.
- Agree the starting and stopping signal, e.g. pointing to a group means they should start and your hand in the air means they stop.

Collective re-enactment 27

- Split the class into small groups. Allocate a sound to each group and give them the appropriate instruments. Include vocal sounds alongside the instruments if children suggest it.
- Using the start and stop signals, give the whole class a short time to practise making their sounds.
- Ask each group to demonstrate their sounds one at a time, to show they understand the start and stop signals.
- Conduct the soundscape like an orchestra, starting and stopping the different groups with the signals. Some groups find it helpful if you name the sounds as you point to them.
- Repeat the soundscape with a few changes, e.g. starting with the quieter sounds, moving to louder ones and finishing with the quieter ones or a few sounds playing at the same time and some pauses.
- Experiment by asking children to select and add repeated words from the description of the setting to the soundscape and perform again with the added words.
- Re-read the description of the setting and/or make a recording asking children to evaluate how well the soundscape reflects that setting.

Reader reflections

Depending on the age and/or maturity of the children:

- Talk about the effects of background sounds and music when watching screen versions of stories and how these can make the reader feel different things. Play a clip of a story with background sounds and/or music as an example.
- Talk about what sounds could be used to create soundscapes of the settings in other familiar stories.

Extension activity

Link to a short extract of classical music that represents a setting and/or characters in a story like *Peter and the Wolf* by Sergei Prokofiev.

EXAMPLE: *THERE'S A RUMBLE IN THE JUNGLE* BY GILES ANDREAE AND DAVID WOJTOWYCZ

Planning and resources

- Children need sight of the book as a stimulus to plan the activity.

Ages 4-6 (EYFS-Year 1)

You will need:

- Percussion instruments with potential to represent the jungle sounds in the book. You need enough for each child to have an instrument.

What to do

- Sit with the children in a semicircle and give one instrument to each child.
- Using the book as a prompt, talk about what sounds you might hear if you walked through the jungle.
- Help the children decide which instruments to use to make the sounds e.g. slowly turning a rain-stick for the whispering trees, banging slowly on a drum for an elephant walking. They can add vocal sounds if appropriate.
- Explain that you will point to the instruments and name the sounds when you want children to play and then raise your hand as a sign to stop, e.g. 'Here come the elephants' – point to those with drums . . . raise hand to stop.
- Children will need to practise this a few times before a final performance.

Reader reflections

Ask:

- 'Do the sounds make you feel like you are in a jungle, like the setting of this book?'
- 'Have we read any other books with jungle settings? Would our soundscape fit the settings in these books too?'

Link to other books about the Jungle.

Extension activities

Record the soundscape and play back to the children to allow them to evaluate its effectiveness in representing the setting.

Link to short extracts of classical music representing animals like those in *Carnival of the Animals* by Camille Saint-Saens.

Further Suggestions

Nen And the Lonely Fisherman by Ian Eagleton and James Mayhew

- Make a soundscape to reflect the more abstract aspects of this story, such as how the characters might be feeling or the atmosphere created by the storm. If appropriate talk about how the storm changes things for the characters.
- Make a soundscape of the storm using vocal sounds and body percussion and/or create twisting and turning dance moves to reflect the waves and perform alongside a recording of the soundscape.

2 Characters and their problems

LINKS TO READING FOR MEANING: dramatising stories; emotional engagement; children articulate what they know and understand; empathy; recalling; retelling; questioning; extending vocabulary; different viewpoints; exploring characters' thoughts, feelings, motives and problems.

Rationale

If we can encourage young children to consider characters and events in rhymes and stories as if they were real, we can begin to move beyond factual recall into a deeper reading for meaning. Imaginary experiences that feel real can facilitate interactions with characters and events in stories and rhymes, giving children a personal relationship with the fiction. When children are asked to deal with problems or consequences of events in nursery rhymes and stories, they become more deeply engaged with the texts and are often keen to offer advice and explain the events to confused minor characters. This helps develop skills of recall and empathy, whilst more analytical strategies like role-on-the-wall help extend vocabulary relating to characters' feelings and suggest different viewpoints.

Contents	
Letters from nursery rhyme characters	30
Spontaneous role play	34
Helping characters in stories	36
Puppets with problems	38
Helping imagined and minor characters	42
Overheard conversations	46
Role-on-the-wall	47

Drama strategies

Hot-seating
Letters from characters
Mantle-of-the-expert

DOI: 10.4324/9781003250777-4

Ages 4-6 (EYFS-Year 1)

Mime
Overheard conversations
Teacher-in-role
Whole group drama

Letters from nursery rhyme characters

Many nursery rhymes conclude with unresolved problems that a group of helpful children might seek to rectify within an imaginary situation, especially if they are sent a letter from a character asking for help. Most of the problems have practical solutions that can be carried out with mimed actions, whilst others require giving advice.

Planning and resources

- Children need to be familiar with the chosen rhyme before the drama.

You will need:

- A letter from one of the characters asking for help (see examples for Little Bo Peep and Humpty Dumpty). Place the letter in the drama space before the drama begins.
- Space for the children to move around.
- A printed copy of the rhyme.

What to do

Stage 1: Set up the imaginary context

- Invite the children to join you in pretending to be in a story.
- Define the space where the story will take place by walking round it. Mention any areas or items in the space that are not part of the story.
- Define the place where you need to be, in the story e.g. in a field or garden and decide on the location of any features needed for the rhyme, e.g. *'Can we pretend there is a broken fence here?'*
- Explain that the story will start when you say the word *'action'* and stop when you say the word *'freeze.'*
- Start the drama/story and ask them to follow you as you walk round. Briefly describe what you see as you walk, e.g. flowers in a garden, a well on a hill or a high wall etc.

Stage 2: introduce a problem or a task

- Discover the letter from the character and read it to the children.
- Keeping in role, use mimed actions to demonstrate how to carry out the work required, e.g. watering the flowers for Mary, so the children understand how to enact the task. Give a general idea of the mimed actions so the children can make up their own versions. If there is more than one job, you can invite suggestions on how to carry out the rest.

Characters and their problems 31

- Join in with the work, giving plenty of praise and encouragement. You can invite cautious or struggling children to help you with your jobs.
- When a few children have finished the task, invite everyone to sit together while you check the work.
- Visit each area where the children were working and ask *'Who has done the work here?'* so you can ask a few questions and give plenty of praise.

Stage 3: Reflection

- Stop the story using the words *'freeze . . . and that is the end of our story.'*
- Ask some questions to encourage reflection, e.g. *'Did you enjoy pretending to be in the story? What part did you like best? What was the hardest job? What do you think (name the character) will say when they find out we have helped?'*
- After the drama write a letter to the children from the character, thanking them for their help.

Extension activities

Children draw themselves carrying out the jobs. Display these alongside a printed copy of the rhyme under the heading *How we helped . . .* or *We were in a story about . . .* Encourage children to talk about their experience as they draw. Invite children to talk about their experience to another adult who didn't take part.

EXAMPLE 1: LITTLE BO PEEP

Text: *Little Bo Peep* **nursery rhyme**
Proceed as previously described, with the following adaptations:

Planning and resources

- Make a copy of the following letter:

    Dear Children,

    Please can you help me. My sheep keep getting lost because the fence round the field where I keep them is broken. I don't have time to fix the fence because I have to keep looking for my sheep.

    I have heard you like to help people. Please will you be very kind and fix the fence round my field, so I can keep my sheep safe.

    You can use the wood and nails, saws and hammers and other tools in the shed in my field.

Ages 4–6 (EYFS–Year 1)

Please work slowly and carefully so no-one gets hurt with the tools.
If you have time, you can paint the fence. You will find tins of red paint and paint brushes on the shelves in the sheds.
You are very kind. Thank you so much.

Love from Little Bo Peep

- Hide the letter from Little Bo Peep somewhere in the room before the children arrive.

What to do

- Show the children a copy of the rhyme in a book or on a poster and invite them to join you in reciting it.
- Ask the children to join you in pretending to be in a story about some children and their teacher who went for a walk in the fields where Bo Peep keeps her sheep.
- Ask the children to pretend that the space you are standing in is Bo Peep's field. Walk round the edge of the field, describing the surrounding broken fence and gate and a shed in the field.
- Starting the drama with the word '*action*,' invite the children to join you as you walk round the field. Point out the broken fence and gate and the shed. Standing on tip toes, pretend to take a look through the shed window and tell the children you can see lots of tools.
- Find the letter and read it to the children.
- Ask the children to watch carefully while you show them what they have to do, to make sure everyone works safely. All your actions need to be mimed, so the children understand that is how they will work. Go to the imaginary shed, open the door, bring out the tools. Ask the children if anyone knows how to repair a fence before making suggestions yourself.
- Read the letter again to check what to do next. Demonstrate how to enter the shed, select a tin of paint, open the lid and stir it with a brush. Ask the children for advice on how best to paint a large fence before offering your own suggestion. Stress the need to work slowly and carefully.
- Invite the children to start work and join in yourself. Give children lots of praise and encouragement. If some children struggle to take part in the drama, ask them to work with you to fix the gate.
- When a few have finished the fence, remind them about the painting.
- When most children have completed some kind of work, ask them to sit together on the grass while you check the work for Bo Peep. Walk along the different parts of the fence, asking which children repaired and painted each part as you go. You are likely to get children claiming to have repaired all of it, but it gives you the opportunity to praise them for their work and kindness.
- Walk everyone out of the field and close the gate. Then stop the drama with the words: '*freeze. And that is the end of our story.*'
- Talk about how kind the children were and ask them which part of the story they liked best.
- Invite the children to join you in reciting the rhyme again.
- Sometime later, send a thank you note to the children from Bo Peep.

Characters and their problems 33

> **Reader reflections**
>
> Ask:
>
> - 'Do we know any other rhymes about sheep or lambs?'
> - 'What colour was the lamb in Mary Had A Little Lamb? That lamb wandered away like Bo Peep's sheep did. Do you remember where it went?'
> - 'Did Little Boy Blue look after any sheep? What happened there?'

EXAMPLE 2: HUMPTY DUMPTY

Texts:
- **The Humpty Dumpty rhyme**
- (Optional) ***Little Lumpty* by Miko Imai**

Proceed as in Example 1, with the following adaptations:

Planning and resources

- Make a copy of the following letter:

    Dear Children

    Please can you help me. Humpty Dumpty fell off my wall yesterday.
    I sent all my horses and all my men to try to fix him back together again but they could not do it.
    Poor Humpty Dumpty is still in pieces by the wall.
    I have heard you are very good at fixing things. Please could you try to fix him back together again.
    I have some glue and other things in the garden sheds that you can use to fix him together.
    Please be very careful when walking round the garden in case you tread on bits of Humpty's broken shell.
    Please send me a note if you manage to fix him. Thank you.
    Best wishes from the king

- Place the letter from the king in the drama space before the children arrive.

What to do

- This works in a similar way to the Little Bo Peep Example 1 but with two differences: There is a need to put Humpty back on the wall after he has been put back together and the safety aspect of sitting on a high wall needs addressing.
- Invite children to join you in obtaining and using imaginary glue and brushes from the shed in the same way as Example 1, but stress the need to tread and work carefully.

- When children have finished the repair, ask them to stand around Humpty so you can inspect the work.
- To mime putting Humpty back on the wall, invite the children to stand in a circle around the imaginary Humpty. Place your hands as if along Humpty's sides and invite the children to do the same. On the words 'One, two, three lift . . .' ask the children to help you lift him onto the wall. Then stand back and look up as if he is on the wall, telling the children what a good job they have done and how pleased the King will be.
- Talk about the dangers of sitting on high walls and ask the children how they could make it safer if Humpty should fall again. Consider the practicality of each suggestion e.g. a mattress would get wet. Pretend to use the tools from the shed to carry out their ideas if they are feasible e.g. planting soft grass or building a pool. If they are not ideas they could carry out at the time, then agree to carry them out later.
- Help the children compose a note to the king telling him what they've done. This could also include safety advice. Then some time later write a thank you note from the King to the children.

Reader reflections

Ask:

- 'Do we know any other rhymes about people falling down like Humpty?'
- 'I know a rhyme about some children who fell down a hill after going to get a pail of water. Do you remember who they were?'
- 'What happened in the rhyme about a baby in a treetop?'

Extension activities

- Re-read the rhyme and a related story such as **Little Lumpty by Miko Imai** and talk about the dangers of walking on high walls.
- Children make safety posters about the dangers of climbing on high walls.

Further Suggestions

Jack and Jill need people to fetch more water from the well.
Mary Mary needs help with her growing garden.
Hush-A-Bye Baby needs a safer place to sleep.

Spontaneous role play

This is a short activity initiated by the teacher, where children spontaneously take on roles as groups of characters linked to a well-known story. Once in role as the characters, they are

Characters and their problems 35

encouraged to articulate their feelings about events and/or discuss solutions to solve some of the problems in the story.

Planning and resources

- Children need to be familiar with the story the characters are in, unless you are adapting it to use as an introduction to a text.

You will need:

- Space for the children to move around.

What to do

- Address the children as if they were the group of characters in the story, asking them to show you something that those characters can do, e.g. '*Witches, show me how you ride your broomsticks.*'
- Introduce an event or a problem for the characters based on the story. Ask them how they feel about the event and/or what they could do to solve the problem.
- Either re-enact the outcome in some way, e.g. via a freeze-frame of the moment or action freeze-narration or read the text to discover or remind them what happened in the story.

EXAMPLE: JACK AND THE BEANSTALK

Planning and resources

You will need:

- A copy of *Jack and the Beanstalk* to read aloud.
- At least two other books the children have read that have giants in them.

What to do

- Address the children as giants and say you have heard that they walk with big steps. Ask them to show you. Ask them for other information about their daily lives such as what big meals they eat etc.
- Tell them you have something important to tell them. A boy called Jack is on his way up a beanstalk to steal things from their castles. Ask them what he might want to take and why. Ask them how they feel about this and what they plan to do about it.
- Enact the solutions using mimed actions if appropriate, e.g. building a wall to keep Jack out, locking up their valuable things.

- Tell them you have to leave and announce that is the end of the story about the giants.
- Ask them if they know a similar story about a boy called Jack and a giant.
- Read the story to the children and compare their experiences as giants with the giant in the story.

> **Reader reflections**
>
> Ask: 'Have we read any other stories about giants? I wonder if any of the giants in the other stories were like the one in Jack and The Beanstalk. I wonder if they lived in a castle in the sky. Let's look at these books to find out.'

Helping characters in stories

Characters in traditional stories can ask for help from the children via a letter in the same way as nursery rhyme characters, but the request is more engaging if it comes directly from a teacher-in-role as a character.

Use the following example as a model for other stories:

EXAMPLE: GOLDILOCKS AND THE THREE BEARS

Planning and resources

- Children need to be familiar with the story prior to the activity and have sight of the story in a book during the activity.

You will need:

- A scarf as a sign of teacher-in-role as Daddy Bear
- A letter from the bears, thanking the children for tidying up the mess.
- Space with enough room for children to move around.
- A paper sign to attach to the wall saying *The Three Bears' House*

What to do

- Attach the sign to the wall of the drama space before the children arrive.
- Read the sign to the children and ask them to pretend you have all been invited to visit the bears' house. Ask them to pretend the room they are in is the bears' house.
- Tell the children you will use the words *'action'* and *'freeze'* to start and stop the story.

Characters and their problems 37

Teacher-in-role

- Tell the children that Daddy Bear was waiting for them when they arrived, but he was looking very sad and worried. Ask the children to pretend that you are Daddy Bear when you wear the scarf. Explain that because you will not speak or look like the bear, they will need to be very good at pretending.
- In role as Daddy Bear, tell the children that Mummy Bear has taken Baby Bear to buy a new chair because a naughty girl called Goldilocks came into your house and broke the chair. Explain briefly how she also ate Baby Bear's porridge and made a mess on the beds with her muddy shoes. Tell them how you need to clear up before Mummy and Baby Bear get back but they might be back soon so there is not enough time. Ask the children if they will be kind enough to help.
- Keeping in role as Daddy Bear, suggest that the children help you wash the floor after the spilt porridge. Pretend to go to a place in the kitchen where the mops and buckets are kept and demonstrate (using mimed actions) how to fill the buckets in the sink, add some cleaner from the cupboard, take a mop and carefully mop the floor. Then let the children carry out the task, along with you.
- When most children have finished, ask them to sit down so you can check the work and thank them for doing such a good job.
- Now pretend to lead the children upstairs to look at the beds. Comment on Goldilocks' muddy shoe marks on the bedding.
- This time describe the jobs, rather than demonstrating them. Ask the children to take off the bed covers, go downstairs and put them in the washing machine in the kitchen, then come back up to put clean covers on the beds from the cupboard in the bedroom. Repeat this so they understand the tasks before they carry out the jobs.
- When most children have completed their jobs, admire the clean bedding and praise the children.
- Lead the children back downstairs and comment on what a lovely surprise it will be when Mummy and Baby Bear return.
- Thank the children and take off the scarf saying 'and Daddy Bear went back into his house looking much happier.'
- Say the word '*freeze*' and tell them you are stopping the story.
- Praise them for their kindness and ask them what work they found the hardest to do.
- Talk about how naughty Goldilocks was and the impact on the Bears.
- Sometime later, send them the thank you letter from the Bears.

Further suggestions for traditional stories

Jack and the Beanstalk: Jack needs help to tidy his garden after the beanstalk came down.

Little Red Riding Hood: Grandma is recovering at Red Riding Hood's house. The woodcutter or neighbour would like to make Grandma's house wolf proof before she returns. It needs a lock on her door, a fence round her house and other ideas from the children to keep any more wolves away.

Figure 2.1 A garden for Snow White

The Elves and the Shoemaker: The shoemaker wants to make new clothes as a surprise for the poor elves who were so kind to him. He has bought some cloth to make the clothes with but he isn't sure what kind of clothes to make and needs help to sew them all. He asks the children for suggestions and asks them to help him sew the tiny clothes before wrapping them up as a surprise.

Snow White and the Seven Dwarves: The dwarves need help to create a garden for Snow White and the prince as a wedding present. Ask the children for ideas on how to make the garden special and meaningful?

Puppets with problems

Children find hand puppets engaging and are only too willing to help the puppets solve any problems they might have. This activity is designed to take place as an introduction to a story. It works best in stories with animal or fantasy characters who have problems, but that doesn't necessarily mean you need a puppet for the main character. You can invent a role for the puppet such as a concerned friend of the main character or someone who might have witnessed the problems and wants to help.

The puppet communicates the problem by whispering to the teacher, who relays what has been said to the children. They then give the puppet advice and/or help if appropriate to the story.

Characters and their problems

Finding the puppet in a sad or confused state increases the children's level of engagement, but it's important to maintain the puppet's responses throughout the activity.

Planning and resources

- Select a story where an animal or creature has a problem to solve.
- Children need access to your chosen story at the end of the drama

You will need:

- A hand puppet that could either be the character with the problem or a friend or eye witness.
- A bed for the puppet such as a shoe box.

What to do

- Invite the children to pretend to be in a story about a puppet. Tell the children that pretending to be in a story is called drama.
- Introduce the words '*action*' and '*freeze*' to start and stop the drama.
- Bring out the puppet and make it appear sad or confused. Ask the children if they can guess how the puppet is feeling and invite one of the children to ask it what is wrong. The puppet then whispers a response to you, so you can tell the children.
- Relay the puppet's problem to the children in stages to encourage them to ask more questions.
- Then ask the children to suggest solutions, giving them an opportunity to talk in pairs first if appropriate.
- Discuss each suggestion seriously. The puppet can listen and agree to consider their ideas.
- After the suggestions have been made, let the puppet thank the children and put it to bed in the box.
- If the children's suggestions don't contradict the existing narrative in the forthcoming story, they can be enacted with mimed actions, but enacting completely different solutions to those in the real story can sometimes confuse children.
- Stop the drama.
- Tell the children you have a book about the puppet's problem.
- Read the book to find out how the problem was solved in the story.

EXAMPLE 1: *FARMER DUCK* BY MARTIN WADDELL

Planning and resources:

- Use this drama activity as an introduction to the book. Children need access to the story at the end of the drama.
- If you have a duck puppet the drama can be about Farmer Duck instead of a friend of his.

Ages 4-6 (EYFS-Year 1)

You will need:

- A hand puppet of a duck or a creature who might live on farm land.
- A bed for the puppet such as a shoe box.
- A large space for the second part of the activity, but if necessary it can be adapted to a smaller area.
- A list of jobs similar to those carried out by Farmer Duck.
- Appropriate images and/or other resources providing information about any of the jobs that may be unfamiliar to the children.

What to do

Introduction (in the classroom)

- Invite the children to pretend to be farmers in a story. Explain that when people pretend to be in a story it's called drama.
- Use the resources to introduce any new vocabulary and talk about the jobs farmers might do every day.
- Tell the children that a puppet would also like to be in the drama. The puppet is in its bed in the box. Explain that when the drama starts, you'll ask the puppet to come out.
- Use the words 'action' and 'freeze' to start and stop or pause the drama.

Part 1 (in the classroom or large space): build belief in the character with a problem

- Start the drama with the puppet looking sad. Ask the children how they think the puppet is feeling. Ask the puppet why he is so sad.
- Let the puppet whisper a response so you can give the children the following information: The puppet is sad because he is very tired. He has been trying to help his friend the duck who has to do all the work on the farm because the farmer will not do anything, but he is now too tired to help any more.
- Suggest that the farmers here might help. The puppet is delighted and reveals all the jobs the duck has to do, checking each time that the farmers know how to do them.
- The puppet rests in the box while the children make a list of jobs.
- Allocate the jobs to the children in groups and make a record of who will do what jobs.
- If you need to move to a larger space, explain to the children that you are pausing the drama to get ready for the next part of the story when the farmers helped with the jobs. Give the children a rough idea when this is likely to take place.

Part 2 (in a large space or a cleared space in the classroom)

- Bring the puppet to the drama space asleep in the box.
- Bring out the list of jobs and remind the children who will do what jobs.
- Before starting the drama, make it clear that all the jobs have to be mimed actions. Give a few examples such as bringing in the cows by waving and shooing them along and then ask children for a few more suggestions on how to mime the actions for the other jobs.

Characters and their problems 41

- Check that everyone knows what job they will do and how they might mime it. Give yourself a job and ask any children who are unsure to help you.
- Explain that everyone needs to do all the jobs at the same time.
- Define the space in the room that will represent the farm and mention any areas out of bounds. Define areas in the room where the farmers can carry out their jobs, e.g. where the cows and sheep are kept and where the house is.
- Restart the drama using the word '*action.*'
- Take a leading role in encouraging the jobs whilst you are doing your own. Praise children who are carrying out their work with commitment rather than commenting on their miming skills.
- Stop the drama when most children appear to have completed their jobs. Ask early finishers to carry out an extra job such as mending a broken gate.
- Talk about how hard the work was and how you now understand why the puppet was so tired.
- Talk about what the duck could do to solve the problem of the lazy farmer.
- Stop the drama on the word '*freeze.*'

Link to the text

- Tell the children you have a story about what happened to the duck.
- Bring out *Farmer Duck* and read it to the children, making reference to the children's work on the farm as appropriate.

Extension activities

- Each child makes a visual record of how they personally helped on the farm. These can be displayed as a record of the work of the whole class, along with a sentence about each.
- Send a thank you letter to the children from the puppet.
- Children read more books about farms.
- Individual children use the puppet to explain to others what happened on the farm.

EXAMPLE 2: *PUMPKIN SOUP* BY HELEN COOPER

Planning and resources

- Use this drama activity as an introduction to the book.

You will need:

- A copy of the text to read aloud to the children after the drama.
- Age appropriate information about how to make soup.

- A hall or enough cleared space in the classroom for children to stand in a circle.
- A puppet of a woodland creature.
- A whiteboard pen and three or four small whiteboards or large sheets of card.

What to do

- Talk about making soup: how to prepare it and how you need to stir and add seasoning etc.
- Ask the children to stand with you in a large circle. Ask them to pretend they are standing around a large pan in which to make enough soup for everyone to share.
- Talk about and demonstrate how to mix, stir and season the soup. Appoint groups to do the different jobs such as seasoning and stirring, emphasising how jobs need to be shared.
- Tell the children you have had a message from a very sad puppet who would like to talk to them. Bring out the puppet who whispers the problem to you, so you can convey the message to the children. Explain the problem as follows: *'The puppet's woodland neighbours were making soup together when they fell out over the jobs. One of them called Duck has run away into the nearby woods and everyone is worried.'* Describe what led up to Duck running away and the particular concerns of his friends as outlined in the book.
- Ask the children what they would say to Duck to persuade him to come home.
- Invite the children to leave messages for the Duck on the trees in case he/she should walk by. These might be words of comfort or advice, but they should represent the children's own words and ideas wherever possible. Prop up the puppet somewhere as you write the children's messages on the whiteboards and read them back to the children to check them.
- Pause the drama. Ask the children to pretend that the trees are around the room. Choose children to stand holding the white boards as if they were the trees with the messages on.
- Restart the drama to take the puppet round the trees to read the messages to Duck. The puppet thanks the children for their help and leaves.
- Read **Pumpkin Soup** to find out what happened to Duck and his friends. Talk about how the friends felt and the falling out.

Extension activities

Link to **A Pipkin of Pepper by Helen Cooper** and read other stories where a character becomes lost or runs away, e.g. **The Best Worst Day Ever by Sophie Henn.**

Helping imagined and minor characters

Many stories have outcomes that have an impact on minor characters or could have an impact on invented characters. In this activity, children assume the role of experts or eye witnesses to the events in a story. They are asked to explain and retell the events to a minor or invented character who is confused or wanting information.

Characters and their problems 43

Sometimes the character can just be someone who is confused about a story they have read, or a minor character seeking clarification about what happened to the other characters, e.g. Grandma asking what the wolf was up to whilst she was locked in the cupboard.

The character is played by the teacher-in-role using a simplified version of the mantle-of-the-expert drama strategy.

Planning and resources

- Children need to be familiar with the chosen story prior to the activity.

You will need:

- A scarf or small item of clothing as a sign of teacher-in-role.

What to do

- Read the story to the children.
- Ask them to pretend you are someone in the story who needs their help.
- Make it clear you will only be that person when wearing the scarf or chosen item of clothing.
- Introduce the words '*action*' and '*freeze*' to start and stop the drama.
- Put on the scarf and take on the role of someone who needs further information about the story.
- When in role as the character, ask searching questions that demand clarity and sequence as the children attempt to retell the story and/or explain the events.
- Thank the children for their help.
- Take off the scarf and stop the drama with the word '*freeze.*'
- Re-read the story or the part of the story relating to the drama and talk about what happened in the drama.

EXAMPLE 1: TELLING A STORY FROM A DIFFERENT PERSPECTIVE

This activity involves telling a story in role as one of the minor characters who did not witness all the events and has questions to ask. Use the following as models for other stories:

The Three Little Pigs: Tell the first part of the story in role as the man who gave the third pig some bricks. Ask the children if they know what happened to the pig after he took away the bricks to build a house.

Little Red Riding Hood:

Either tell the story as if you were Grandma. Relate the events up to the point where you were locked in the cupboard. You want to know what the wolf was doing while you were in the cupboard before Red Riding Hood arrived. Then pick up the story from when you were let out of the cupboard.

Or tell the story as if you were the woodman who rescued Red Riding Hood and let Grandma out of the cupboard. You want to know why the wolf was dressed in Grandma's clothes and how he found out where Grandma lived.

EXAMPLE 2: MAISIE/MICKY MUDDLE

This example is a version of mantle-of-the-expert where children play the role of those who know more than the character played by the teacher-in-role. The character known here as Maisie or Micky Muddle makes mistakes for children to correct when telling a familiar story. Children usually enjoy this teacher/pupil role reversal and pay close attention to the details of the story in order to correct any mistakes.

Planning and resources

- Select a story the children are familiar with and plan mistakes for the children to correct. Simple substitutions work well to start with e.g. *Goldilocks and the four bears*, adding more subtle mistakes as appropriate. You can also plan to get the details mixed up with other familiar stories such as the bears climbing a beanstalk etc

You will need:

- A scarf to play the part of Maisie or Micky Muddle.

What to do

- Ask the children to pretend you could be someone else when wearing the scarf. Explain that you would like to pretend to be someone called Maisie/Micky Muddle who likes telling stories but keeps getting in a muddle.
- Talk about what the word *muddle* means and how they might have to help Maisie/Micky Muddle to tell the story.
- Put on the scarf and in role as Maisie/Micky Muddle offer to tell the children a story but explain that you often get stories muddled up so might need some help.
- Start the story and pause after your first mistake. If the children don't correct you, then tell them you think you may have got something wrong and ask them if they know what it is. Children are likely to correct you most of the time, but if not then you can suddenly remember the correct version for that particular error and move on to the next one.
- Take off the scarf at the end of the story and remind the children that you are no longer Maisie/Micky Muddle.
- Praise them for helping the character and remark on how well they know the story.

Characters and their problems 45

- Despite the fact that you have just played the role, children will usually accept that you were not there as their teacher, so you can try feigning ignorance to ask them what mistakes Maisie/Micky Muddle made.
- You can use this character again to tell other stories.

EXAMPLE 3: *ALIENS LOVE UNDERPANTS* BY CLAIRE FREEDMAN AND BEN CORT

Proceed as in the overview of the section 'Helping imagined and minor characters,' with the following adaptations:

Planning and resources

You will need:

- A copy of the book to read to the children.
- A scarf as a sign of teacher-in-role.

What to do

- Read the story to the children.
- Use the scarf to set up teacher-in-role as someone who has had underpants stolen from their washing line. Describe how you felt when you went to get the washing in and found all the underpants had gone.
- Ask the children if they know where your underpants could have gone.
- Ask the children for suggestions on how to stop this happening again and consider each idea.
- Thank the children, then take off the sign of role and use the word '*freeze*' to stop the drama.
- Re-read the story and talk about how the children helped.

Reader reflections

Sit with the children close to the book corner in your classroom or if this is not possible then display some books nearby. Ask the children if they enjoyed the story and if they found it funny. Ask the children if there are any funny stories or poems in their book corner. Have a few visible that you can refer to. Use this as an opportunity to talk about different kinds of books in the book corner such as funny books, scary books, books that tell you about things etc.

Further Suggestions

If You Come to Earth by Sophie Blackall

Role play a visitor from outer space who has come to earth asking questions about the planet. Ask similar questions to those in the book.

Handa's Surprise by Eileen Browne

Role play Handa's neighbour who thinks Handa must have made a mistake about the changing fruit. The neighbour doesn't understand how anything like that could have happened. What do the children think?

The Very Hungry Caterpillar by Eric Carle

Role play a gardener whose fruit was eaten by the Very Hungry Caterpillar. Ask the children if they know who ate the fruit and asks for advice on how to protect the garden from more caterpillars.

Jack and The Beanstalk

Role play Jack's neighbour who wants to know why there was a huge beanstalk in Jack's garden that has now fallen down. Do the children know anything about it?

The Lighthouse Keeper's Lunch by Ronda and David Armitage

Role play a shopkeeper who is curious to know why Mrs. Grinling bought so many large jars of extra strong mustard when she came for her weekly shop. Have the children got any idea why?

Elmer by David McKee

Role play a visitor who can't understand why all the elephants are painted different colours on Elmer Day except Elmer. Do the children know why?

Lost and Found by Oliver Jeffers

Role play the man in the Lost and Found Office who wants to know if the boy ever found anyone who had lost the penguin. Do the children know what happened?

Overheard conversations

Planning and resources

- Choose a character from a familiar story to have a one-sided phone conversation revealing some of the events in the story. These could be minor characters or invented

characters linked to the story such as someone living close to the bridge in The Three Billy Goats Gruff story phoning a friend.
- Decide on where the character is placed and at what point in the story they are making the call, e.g. in a house overlooking the bridge where the troll is waiting, just before the first little Billy Goat tries to cross.

You will need:

- A scarf or similar item as a sign of teacher-in-role.

What to do

- Read the story to the children.
- Ask them to pretend you are a different person when you wear the scarf.
- Ask them to pretend they can hear that person talking on the phone.
- Invite the children to listen to the conversation in order to find out who that person is, who they might be talking to and what they are talking about.
- Introduce the words *'action'* and *'freeze'* to start and stop the drama.
- Put on the scarf to take on the role and pick up an imaginary phone. Hold a conversation on the phone giving clues about the story without making things too specific. The amount of information and challenge you offer will depend on the age and confidence of the children. A simple conversation for younger children about the Three Billy Goats story might go like this:

   Hello. Listen. I have something important to tell you. There's a nasty troll living under the bridge near my house. This morning when I looked out of my window, I saw three animals on the other side of the bridge waiting to cross. I'm not sure what they are because they are too far away but one is very small. I think the grass is better over here but I'm worried the troll might eat them. . . . Yes I know you are busy. . . . Just come as soon as you can. . . . That troll is very dangerous but I'm sure you will know how to scare it away. Thank you Bye.

- Use the word *'freeze'* to stop the conversation and take off the scarf to come out of role.
- Ask the children to think about who and where your character on the phone might be, who they could be talking to and what they were talking about and then perform the conversation again so they can check.
- If appropriate let the children talk in pairs before sharing their answers to your questions.
- Accept all ideas and possibilities that could fit with the story. For example in the *Three Billy Goats Gruff*, the person on the other end of the phone could be the police, a friend or a farmer etc.

Role-on-the-wall

Planning and resources

- Select a main character from a story and draw a large outline of the character on a sheet of paper or on a screen. You can use a basic human outline or head and shoulders if it's a person, or a simplified outline for an animal or creature.

You will need:

- A copy of the story.
- (Optional) A bank of simple words to describe a character, including some which would not fit the character depicted on your role-on-the-wall.

What to do

- Place the outline on the wall or on a screen.
- Read the story to the children or remind them of the events and write the name of the character below the outline.
- Ask the children what they know about the character from the story and write these comments inside the role-on-the-wall. Ask them how they know this and encourage reference to the text. Refer to some of the words from the word bank if you use one. You can use symbols or pictures in addition to or instead of the words if more appropriate.
- Using a word bank and/or children's own suggestions, write what the children **think** of the role-on-the-wall character around the outside of the outline.
- If appropriate you can create another role-on-the-wall for another character in the story and record what they think of each other along arrows drawn between them.

Extension activity

Use a simple form of hot-seating.
Ask: 'What else would you like to know about this character and what questions would you ask if you could meet them?'
Agree on some appropriate questions and choose a confident child to ask the first question. Explain that you will pretend to be a different person when you sit on a chair known as the hot-seat. Sit on the hot-seat and introduce yourself as a friend or acquaintance of the character who will try to answer their questions. After the hot-seating, ask the children to summarise what new things they have found out about the character.

EXAMPLE: CINDERELLA

Planning and resources

You will need:

- A role-on-the-wall outline to represent Cinderella and one outline to represent her sisters.
- A bank of simple words to describe characters, including some that relate to the story, e.g. hard-working, naughty, good, greedy, kind, unkind, tired, jealous, careful, mean, sad, angry, upset, happy, cruel, lazy, beautiful, dirty.

What to do

- Read the story to the children or remind them of the events.
- Use the children's own suggestions and words from the word bank to write words to describe Cinderella inside the role-on-the-wall outline.
- Introduce the sisters outline and add words to describe them inside their outline.
- Draw an arrow from the sisters to Cinderella and write words and phrases along it to describe what the sisters feel about her.
- Create further discussion with the following questions:

    'What should the sisters do at the end of the story? Should they say sorry, send a note, offer to work for Cinderella. What should Cinderella do?'

Further Suggestions

- Little Red Riding Hood and the wolf. Write what the wolf thinks of her, e.g. that she is silly, tasty or foolish.
- Goldilocks. Write facts inside the outline and children's opinions on the outside.
- The Gruffalo in **Julia Donaldson's *The Gruffalo*.** Write facts inside and children's opinions outside.
- The Highway Rat in **Julia Donaldson's** book ***The Highway Rat***. Write facts inside and children's opinions outside.
- Create a role-on-the-wall for a creature linked to information books such as a mini-beast, sea creature, dinosaur or jungle animal.

3 Freezing key moments

LINKS TO READING FOR MEANING: dramatising stories; engaging with a text; questioning; empathy; recalling; sequencing; exploring key moments; exploring characters' thoughts and feelings; inference; predictions; comparisons across texts; and conversations about books.

Rationale

This chapter focuses on ways in which a simple drama strategy such as a freeze-frame can support a deeper exploration of a text. Most children are familiar with the concept of a paused image on screen and are able to grasp the idea of a freeze-frame representing a frozen moment.

The need to depict an authentic representation of a text in a freeze-frame provides the motivation to search for meaning within that text, with opportunities for a teacher to model how to make inferences and predictions. The shared discussion involved in creating a freeze-frame creates significant opportunities for language development. The physical representation of a text in a freeze-frame also helps bring the text to life.

Contents

A Key Moment	51
Images	54
Beginning, middle and end	55
Predictions and alternatives	57
Bringing frames to life	58
Comparisons across texts	59

Drama strategies

Forum theatre
Freeze-frame
Improvisation

DOI: 10.4324/9781003250777-5

A key moment

Planning and resources

- Children need to be familiar with the chosen text or extract beforehand and have sight of the text during the activity.
- Select a significant moment from the text involving two to four characters.
- Plan two alternatives for where each character might be looking and why.
- Plan two alternatives for what each character might be thinking and why. (Optional)

You will need:

- One A4 sized card with a heart-shaped outline (a Feelings Heart).
- One A4 sized card with a Thought Bubble outline (optional).
- One small item to represent each character e.g. a scarf, apron, waistcoat or simple mask.
- A cleared space at the front of the group.

What to do

- Explain the idea of a freeze-frame to the children and the moment you have chosen e.g. *'I wonder what this moment might look like in a freeze -frame. Let's see.'*
- Choose the group of children who will make the freeze-frame and invite them to wear the items to indicate their characters if they wish, although this should not be obligatory.
- Describe the setting for the freeze-frame and indicate the position of any key features e.g. *'Can we pretend this is The Three Bears' kitchen and over here is the door to the forest?'*

Where are the characters looking?

- Ask the first character to stand in the frame and say: *'I wonder where that character is likely to be **looking**.'* Voice your alternatives aloud to model a thoughtful response with reference to what is known in the text. Then ask the class for their suggestions. If appropriate, ask the children to talk to a partner before collecting their suggestions.
- Refer to the text for evidence to back up each of the children's suggestions before the final decision is made. Children in the actual freeze-frame should also take part in the discussions.
- Ask the character to look in the agreed direction.
- Use the same process with the other characters to select an appropriate orientation for each.
- Before making a **draft freeze-frame** to show the agreed positions of the characters, remind the characters where they need to look and give a reminder of the moment and a countdown: *'This is what it might have looked like when . . . . . . 1-2-3-freeze . . . . Hold it . . . 1-2-3-relax.'*

Ages 4-6 (EYFS-Year 1)

How are the characters feeling?

- Hold the heart-shaped outline (Feelings Heart) over each character in turn to ask how they might be feeling. Ask for alternatives to words like happy or sad and refer to the text where necessary. When a decision has been made, ask the children in the class to use their bodies to show how each character might look when feeling that way. If using masks, focus on hands and body.
- Re-make the freeze-frame, asking the characters to use their faces and/or bodies to express the feelings.

(Optional) What are the characters thinking?

- Use the same process as the Feelings Heart to introduce the Thought Bubble.
- As you hold the Thought Bubble above each character, voice your alternatives on what each character might be thinking and why and then ask the children for their suggestions.
- If appropriate, make the freeze-frame again, asking the characters to speak out their thoughts in turn or write them down so you can read them out.

> **Extension activities**
>
> Children make a story box to depict the scene or make cards folded into three sections so they stand up, with a drawing of the scene in the middle and sentences about the scene on the outer sections.

EXAMPLE: GOLDILOCKS AND THE THREE BEARS

Planning and resources

- Children need sight of the part of the text where Goldilocks is about to run out of the Bears' house, pursued by the Bears.

You will need:

- One small item to represent each of the characters, e.g. an apron for Goldilocks and a toy or a bib for Baby Bear.
- One Feelings Heart.
- One Thought Bubble (optional).
- A cleared performance space for a small group.

What to do

- Introduce the freeze-frame as previously described, focusing on the moment when Goldilocks is about to run out of the house, pursued by the Bears.
- Choose four children to represent the characters in the freeze-frame and invite them to put on the items of clothing as signs of role if they wish.
- Give options as you ask the children to decide on where each character might be looking e.g.:

    Is Goldilocks looking into the forest because she is scared and wants to get away or is she looking back, feeling sorry for what she has done? What has just happened in the story? How might she be feeling and what might she do if she is feeling like that?

    Is Daddy Bear looking at Goldilocks because he wants to catch her or is he looking at the broken chair and Baby Bear's empty bowl because he needs to tidy up?

    Is Baby Bear looking at Goldilocks because he is cross or at his broken chair?

    Is Mummy Bear looking at Goldilocks because she wants to catch her or is she looking somewhere else?

- Use the Feelings Heart for each of the characters.
- Use the Thought Bubble if appropriate for the age and concentration level of the class.

Extension activities

- Children draw the moment depicted in the freeze-frame and write a sentence or two below it to describe what is happening. Alternatively they can write inside adhesive Thought Bubbles and/or Feelings Hearts positioned above the drawings of the characters.
- Record the moment digitally and display with written Thought Bubbles and/or Feelings Hearts, dictated by the class.

Further Suggestions

Room on the Broom by Julia Donaldson

Freeze the moment the dragon saw the *horrible beast*. Using the illustration as a guide, invite a group of children to stand crouched together like the characters, to represent the illusion of the beast. Then add the witch and the dragon.

Dogger by Shirley Hughes

Freeze the moment Dogger had just been bought by the little girl.

Little Red Riding Hood

Freeze the moment Little Red Riding Hood told the wolf where she was going.

Jack and the Beanstalk

Freeze the moment Jack brought beans back to his mother after selling the cow.

Snow White

Freeze the moment the huntsman left Snow White in the forest.

Images

Planning and resources

- Select one to three images depicting key moments in a story book, picture book or information book e.g. people taking part in a festival or celebration. These can be illustrations, cartoons or photos.
- Children will need sight of these chosen images during the activity, with access to the text when necessary.

You will need:

- A Feelings Heart
- A Thought Bubble (optional)
- A cleared performance space.

What to do

- Read the book to the children and draw their attention to the images.
- Introduce the idea of a freeze-frame to represent one or some of the images.
- Make it clear that the freeze-frames will not look exactly the same as the images.
- Proceed as in 'a key moment' but the direction in which the characters are looking will already be set, so focus on how the characters' bodies can be positioned in a similar way to the images.
- Use a Feelings Heart to think about how the characters are likely to be feeling, based on the information in the text and then use a Thought Bubble if appropriate.

EXAMPLE 1: *LIGHTING THE LAMP:* **A DIWALI STORY BY JONNY ZUCKER: FESTIVAL TIME**

Proceed as in 'a key moment,' with the following adaptations:

- Select three images from the book to make freeze-frames of key moments in the festival of Diwali:

1   Listening to the story of Rama and Sita
2   Helping to make food or exchanging gifts and sweets
3   Lighting Diva lamps

- Use the Feelings Heart and look at the images for clues about how each person might be feeling about the event taking place. Encourage the children to think of different feelings other than happy e.g. the grandma might feel pleased to teach the child how to make the food, the girl might feel proud to make the food and the boy watching might feel hungry.
- Finally make the freeze-frames of the images.
- If you can take a photo of each freeze-frame, children can compare them to the images in the book.

Beginning, middle and end

What to do

- Proceed as in 'a key moment,' but select three key moments, one from the beginning, one from the middle and one from the end of a story to provide a sequence of events.
- Simple masks can be used to depict animals or imaginary creatures in the freeze-frames if required.

EXAMPLE 1: THE CHRISTMAS NATIVITY

Text: *Lion Bible Favourites for the Very Young*, compiled by Lois Rock

What to do

- Create freeze-frames of the following key moments from the Christmas Nativity story using basic costumes and props:
    1   The angels appear to the shepherds. In this freeze-frame, three children can represent the angels whilst the rest of the class represent the shepherds.
    2   The three kings' journey to the star with their gifts.
    3   The stable scene with the baby, Mary, Joseph and a couple of stable animals.
- Use Feelings Hearts and Thought Bubbles as appropriate.
- If you take photographs of each freeze-frame they can be displayed as a sequence with accompanying captions.

Extension activity

This can be presented as a whole school Christmas Nativity performance, with a teacher narrating between the freeze-frames.

56 *Ages 4–6 (EYFS–Year 1)*

EXAMPLE 2: THE STORY OF RAMA AND SITA

Text: *Rama and Sita: The Story of Diwali* **by Malachy Doyle and Christopher Corr**

What to do

- Proceed as in Example 1, but with three key moments from the story of Rama and Sita e.g.:

    1 Rama travels through the forest searching for Sita.
    2 Rama asks the Monkey King for help.
    3 Rama and Sita are crowned king and queen.

- Include all the children in the class as the people watching the ceremony for the freeze-frame of the last scene.
- Use simple masks or small items of clothing to indicate the characters.

> ### Extension activity
>
> This can be performed with intervening narration as in Example 1.

Figure 3.1 Rama asks the monkey king for help

Predictions and alternatives

What to do

Proceed as in 'a key moment,' with the following adaptations:

Predictions:

- After working with a partner to collect ideas, ask the children to work with you to create a class freeze-frame to depict a prediction of what happens next following a key moment in the story or what might happen based on the title and image on the cover. You can also use this to speculate on what might happen to the characters after the story has finished.
- You can make two freeze-frames to show different predictions.
- Older or more confident children can work in groups to produce their own freeze-frame predictions to share with the class.

Alternatives

- Pause before the end of the story and work with the children to create two freeze-frames to show alternative endings before reading the ending in the book.
- If appropriate to the story, work with the class to create two freeze-frames to show characters located in two different places during the story and explore what they feel about the same incident.

EXAMPLE: *LOST AND FOUND* BY OLIVER JEFFERS

What to do

- Read the story to the children up to the point where the boy says goodbye to the penguin and ask the children why they think the penguin was so sad. Then read on to where the boy realises he has made a *big mistake* and ask them what that mistake was.

Either

- Ask the children what they think might happen after the boy realises his mistake. Select one or two predictions to explore through freeze-frames. If children are unsure about what to predict, prompt them with some *'What might happen if'* questions.

or

- Work with the children to create one freeze-frame showing the boy's thoughts and feelings when he realised his mistake and another showing the penguin with his thoughts and feelings. Then ask the children to predict what happens next.

- Finally read the rest of the story to the children. Ask: 'Was this what we expected? How do you feel about that?'
- If their predictions were different from those in the story, talk about how their ideas could make another similar story with a different ending.

Bringing frames to life

Planning and resources

- Choose a moment from a story with potential for further dialogue between characters.

You will need:

- One A4 speech bubble.
- A performance space.
- A copy of the text.

What to do

- Choose children who are confident speakers to represent the characters.
- Make a freeze-frame as in 'a key moment' but with more focus on the feelings of the characters.
- Once the freeze-frame has been performed, hold the speech bubble over each character in turn and talk about what they might say if the moment were brought to life for a few seconds. The intention is to give the characters a rough idea of what to say rather than giving them the exact words.
- Agree an order of speaking and bring the freeze-frame to life for a few seconds or until every character has spoken. Then freeze the moment to finish. Some children need a few attempts at this.
- If appropriate ask the class to work in pairs to improvise their version of the conversation. Children can then be invited to share how they felt when they played these characters in their pairs.
- Invite the children to predict or recall what happened next before reading the text to find out.
- If appropriate, talk about similar incidents in real life.

Reader reflections

Ask:

- 'How did it make you feel when you read this part of the story?'
- 'What kind of story is this?'

'Is it a happy story or a sad story, a sad story with a happy ending, a funny or a scary story [adapt this question to suit the children]*?'*
Link this conversation to reading for pleasure by inviting the children to share the kinds of stories they enjoy reading.

EXAMPLE: *DOGGER* BY SHIRLEY HUGHES

What to do

Proceed as previously described, with the following adaptions:
- Read the story to the children up to and including the point where Bella runs after the little girl to ask her to give Dogger back.
- Freeze the moment depicted in the illustration and after collecting suggestions from the class, bring it to life to improvise the words Bella said and the response of the little girl.
- Freeze again after the conversation when both children begin to cry. Explore the thoughts and feelings of both characters in this second freeze.
- If appropriate, invite the children to work in pairs to improvise their version of the conversation, freezing at the point where they both start to cry.
- Invite children to talk about how they felt when playing these characters.
- Ask the children to predict what happened next or recall what happened if they are already familiar with the story.

Comparisons across texts

Planning and resources

- Select at least two texts with similar characters or aspects e.g. a wedding at the end of two fairy tales, two stories with a witch who makes a spell or two stories where a character runs away or becomes lost.
- Choose a key moment from each text that will reveal the similarities.

What to do

- Read one of the texts to the children or remind them of the events if it's a familiar story.
- Work with the class to make a freeze-frame from one of your chosen texts. Make the freeze-frame in a similar way to 'a key moment.'

- Repeat with the other text using a different group of children to make this second freeze-frame.
- Now re-make the two freeze-frames side by side.
- Ask the children if they can pick out anything that is the same or similar in the freeze-frames.
- Then ask them to pick out any key differences.

EXAMPLE: STORIES WITH A WOLF

Texts

- **The Three Little Pigs**
- **Little Red Riding Hood**
- **There Is No Big Wolf in This Story by Lou Carter**

What to do

- Proceed as previously described, to make the following two freeze-frames: the moment when the wolf tried to blow down the house of straw in *The Three Little Pigs* and the moment the wolf arrived at Granny's House in *Little Red Riding Hood*.
- Focus on the role of the wolf in both stories to work out any similarities and differences.
- Read **There Is No Big Wolf in This Story by Lou Carter** and link to the work with the freeze-frames.

Further Suggestions

- Create two freeze-frames based on stories with dragons and link to **There Is No Dragon in This Story by Lou Carter.**

4 An imaginary experience

LINKS TO READING FOR MEANING: emotional engagement with texts; vocabulary linked to topic books; exploring themes; making comparisons across texts.

Rationale

An imaginary experience allows children to explore aspects of a story or topic book prior to reading the text. It brings the books to life and provides children with an opportunity to engage with the meaning of the texts on a more personal level after having shared a similar experience. You can also tailor the experiences in the drama to reflect those in the text, allowing children to compare their experiences with those in the books.

It often takes the form or an imaginary journey or visit to a place linked to the books. Using teacher-in-role deepens the experience, often introducing a problem linked to the story or topic.

Contents	
A pet dragon	61
Journey to topical places	64
Caring for the environment	66

Drama strategies

Actions
Dramatic play
Teacher as narrator
Teacher-in-role
Whole group drama

A pet dragon

This activity is designed as an introduction to the many stories featuring baby dragons, but the dragon could be replaced by another baby creature with an important role in a story.

DOI: 10.4324/9781003250777-6

Children are invited to join the teacher in creating and caring for their own pet dragon, resulting in subsequent comparisons between their dragons and those in the story. This creates a personal link to the text which facilitates a deeper engagement with the story.

The success of this activity relies on the teacher's ability to build belief in the existence of the dragons, as a model for the children.

Suggested Texts:

- *Ten Minutes to Bed Little Dragon* by Rhiannon Fielding
- *Me and My Dragon* by David Biedrzycki
- *There's A Dragon in Your Book* by Tom Fletcher
- *When a Dragon Comes to Stay* by Caryl Hart
- *My Dragon Book Series* by Steve Herman
- *Dilwyn the Welsh DRAGON* by Samuel Langley Swain
- Descriptions of the baby dragon in *Mimi and the Mountain Dragon* by Michael Morpurgo

Planning and resources

- Children will need access to your chosen story or stories about baby dragons after the drama.

You will need:

- A space large enough for children to move around.
- Images of dragons.

What to do

- Share the images of the dragons and talk about their habits etc. Suggest that not all dragons are dangerous, especially baby dragons.
- Tell the children you are going to pretend to be in a story where you have a baby dragon to look after.
- Using mimed actions, stroke a sleeping baby dragon on your lap. Describe how small it is and although it has tiny teeth and gives out tiny puffs of smoke from its nostrils, it has a kind face and is not dangerous.
- Ask the children for advice on what to call it, what it might eat and how to look after it.
- Ask the children to join you in the story by pretending to have a baby dragon each, so your dragon will have some friends to play with. Most children will be keen to create their own dragon, but if any child appears particularly anxious, suggest they help you look after your dragon.
- Invite the children to gently stroke the sleeping dragons on their laps and ask them how it feels.
- Ask them to think of a name for their dragon and tell a talk partner.
- Share the problem that the dragons need somewhere safe to sleep, as they can't stay on laps all day.

An imaginary experience 63

- Ask for suggestions on what they could sleep on. Gently put the sleeping dragons on the floor while you prepare beds for them. Try to keep in role if the children make any changes e.g. if a child tells you their dragon has woken up, suggest you put a collar and lead on the dragons so you can tie them up safely whist you prepare the beds.
- Ask them to find a space in the room where they can make a bed for their dragon and find a space for your own. Manage the activity by giving a commentary as you make the bed for your dragon based on the children's suggestions e.g. *'What did we say we could use for a bed? Yes let's do that.'*
- When the beds are ready, ask children to collect their dragons and put them to bed.
- Talk about all the other things you will need to do, like putting out bowls for water and food, washing the dragon, taking it for a walk. Talk about playing with the dragons and what toys they could have.
- Wake up the dragons to carry out the tasks. Depending on the confidence of the children, either complete these tasks together as before or invite the children to complete them on their own. Whatever method you choose, allow time for children to play with their dragons on their own, using the toys they have thought of.
- When children begin to lose interest, announce that it's time to put the dragons in their beds, as they will be tired. Then creep away out of the room or to another area.
- Ask the children to listen carefully as you tell them what happened next in their story about the baby dragons. Then narrate a suitable ending e.g.:

The baby dragons loved the children and their teacher, but after a while they grew too big for their beds. They knew they would grow even bigger and couldn't stay. So one day they spread their wings, breathed out a puff of fire and flew off into the sky to join all the other grown up dragons. But the baby dragons never forgot the kind children and their teacher who looked after them so well.

- Ask the children what they liked best about looking after their baby dragon and share your own thoughts.

Link to the text

- Invite them to listen to a story about a baby dragon and read the chosen story.
- Invite comparisons between their dragons and those in the story.
- Link to other stories about baby dragons.

Reader reflections

Ask:

- *'Which do you like the best, stories about baby dragons or stories about grown up dragons? Why do you think that?'*
- *'Do you like stores about gentle dragons or scary dragons? Why do you think that?'*

> **Extension activity**
>
> Children draw and label their dragons and/or their toys for dragons and contribute to writing an information book on *How to look after a Baby Dragon*.

Journey to topical places

Imaginary journeys can be via any transport such as a bus, train, plane, space ship, submarine or even a magic carpet. They can take children on a journey to photograph or explore places linked to topics such as farms, outer space or even under the sea, where they come across problems to solve or characters to help. Journeys can be used as a dramatic holding form, with children going to a new destination each time you use it.

Use the following example of a journey to photograph creatures in the jungle as a model for other stories.

EXAMPLE: A JUNGLE JOURNEY

Texts:

- *Walking Through the Jungle* by Julie Lacome
- *A Rumble in the Jungle* by Giles Andreae
- *Dear Zoo* by Rod Campbell

Planning and resources

You will need:

- Space for children to move around.
- A small item of clothing such as a scarf or waistcoat as a sign of teacher-in-role.
- Images of jungle creatures.

What to do

- Talk about the images of the jungle creatures and invite the children to join you in pretending to go on a journey through a jungle to take photos of the creatures there.
- Walk round the space to indicate where the jungle will be and mention any items or areas that are not in the story.
- Use the words '*action*' and '*freeze*' to start and stop the drama at any point.
- Start the drama and invite the children to copy you as you pretend to pack an imaginary backpack for the jungle journey. Pack a camera and a bottle of water and ask the children what else they should put in their small jungle back packs.

An imaginary experience

- Put the packed bag on your back and pretend to apply sun cream, inviting the children to do the same.
- After advising everyone to put on a sunhat, tell the children they have a rowing boat each, to row down the river into the jungle. Step into your imaginary boat, take up the oars and invite the children to do the same with their own boats.
- Row on the spot to indicate travel and suggest you all sing a song such as *Row, Row Row Your Boat* as you row along.
- Announce you have arrived in the jungle and ask the children to keep quiet so they don't scare the animals away. Suggest you carefully step out of the boats, tie them up and stand together on the land.
- Tell the children to take out their cameras and follow you to a place where there are monkeys to photograph. Walk a short way and then stop to indicate there are monkeys in the distance. Tell the children to take photos of the monkeys and then come back. This is likely to be very quick.
- Repeat this with another place where there are two kinds of creatures to photograph such as parrots and elephants. When they return, ask them if they managed to photograph both creatures.
- Sit the children down for a rest and a drink from their imaginary water bottles.
- Stop the drama and move time on with the words *'Listen carefully. I am now going to tell you what happened next in the story.'*
- Narrate your way into teacher-in-role by saying:

'As the children sat drinking their water, someone arrived to speak to them. I'd like to pretend to be that person when I am wearing this scarf. When I take it off again I will come back to being myself. Is that OK?'

- Put on the scarf to play the part of someone in the jungle looking for a creature to take home for a pet. Ask them if an elephant would make a good pet and then talk about the possibility of other creatures as listed in your chosen texts such as **Dear Zoo**. Encourage the children to give reasons why each creature would not make a good pet. Ask for advice about what animals would make good pets, then thank the children for their help. Ask them what they have been doing in the jungle and ask if they think it's better to take photos than take animals away from the jungle for pets. Thank them and leave.
- Take off the scarf saying, *'and the person looking for pets went away.'*
- Restart the drama. Either ask the children what the person said – they will accept this if you say it with conviction – or make a positive comment about the advice. Then suggest you go back to the boats.
- Sing the song again as you return home on the boats and stop the drama.
- Ask the children what parts of the story they liked best and talk about the advice they gave the person looking for a pet.
- Read a relevant text like **Dear Zoo by Rod Campbell** and link with the events on their jungle journey.

Reader reflections

Ask:

- 'Do you enjoy reading books about jungle animals?'
- 'Do you have a favourite jungle animal you like to read about?'

    Share some examples of books about jungle animals and if appropriate ask children if they can find any more in the book corner.

Extension activities

- Link to the theme of appropriate pets in *I Want a Pet* by **Lauren Child**
- Children draw the photos they took on the jungle journey.

Caring for the environment

Children can go on imaginary visits to enact some of the activities linked to topic books. They can then be presented with issues or problems relating to the topic, such as caring for the environment. You can make the activity longer by combining it with an imaginary journey.

Use the following examples as models for other imaginary day trips linked to the class topic:

EXAMPLE 1: KEEPING THE SEASIDE CLEAN

Suggested Texts:

- ***A Day at the Seaside: Hattie and Friends* by Lesley Berrington**

    If you are linking the drama to this inclusive book, you can ensure that the children experience some of the same activities enjoyed by the characters. These can include the sounds and smells of the seaside mentioned by the little girl Lucy, who has a visual impairment.

- ***Meet the Oceans* by Caryl Hart**
- ***Somebody Swallowed Stanley* by Sarah Roberts**
- ***Clem and Crab* by Fiona Lumbers**
- ***Clean Up* by Nathan Bryon**
- ***Harry Saves the Ocean* by Sylva Fae and N. G. K.**
- ***What the Ladybird Heard at the Seaside* by Julia Donaldson**
- ***The Blue Giant* by Katie Cottle**

An imaginary experience

Planning and resources

- Children need to be aware of seaside activities and related vocabulary.

You will need:

- A card with a sign saying '**open**' on one side and '**closed**' on the reverse.
- A sign saying '**café.**'
- An apron or overall as a sign of teacher-in-role.
- A space big enough for the children to move around freely.

What to do

- Place the **café** sign on a wall and put the **open/closed** sign and the apron/overall close by.
- Invite the children to join you in pretending to be in a story about some children and their teacher who go to the seaside. Talk about what they might see and do there. Invite children to share their own experiences if appropriate.
- Ask them to pretend that the room is the seaside and the sign on the wall is where the seaside café is. Point out the direction of the sea.
- Use the words '*action*' and '*freeze*' to start and pause or stop the drama when necessary.
- Start the drama by pretending to put on your sun hat and sun cream and invite the children to do the same. Use mimed actions throughout the drama as a model for the children.
- Ask for suggestions on what to pack in your beach bags, such as a towel to sit on and a bucket and spade etc. before packing them. Use this as an opportunity to mention how we must be careful if we take anything in plastic bags, because they can be dangerous for creatures living beside or in the sea.
- Ask them to pick up their bags and walk with you down to the beach.
- After a short time walking, suggest you all sit on the sand to decide what activity to do first.
- Discuss what to do then pretend to carry out various beach activities such as digging, making sand castles, collecting stones etc. Add activities the children will read about in the book(s) you have chosen. Try to involve the children in deciding what to do next each time. Include paddling but notice a flag on the beach telling you it's not safe to go swimming. Use this as an opportunity to talk briefly about beach safety.
- Suggest you all go to the café garden for something to eat and direct them to sit by the **café** sign. Mention all the litter blowing around in the café garden and how unpleasant it is. Then notice a small bird entangled in a plastic bag. Ask the children to keep very still so as not to scare the bird. Creep towards it and gently release the bird from the bag, describing what you are doing as you do so. Watch the bird fly away and then bring the bag back. Look for a bin to put it in and notice there are a few in the café garden.
- Pause the drama.

- Ask the children to pretend you are the café owner when you put on the apron or overall.
- Put on the clothing to take on the role and pick up the **open /closed** sign. In role as the café owner, show the children the '**closed**' side and explain that you have to close the café garden because litter and rubbish have blown into the garden from the beach, including plastic bags that could blow into the sea. Ask them if they have ever seen any creatures stuck in plastic bags and encourage them to share details of the rescue. Explain more about why plastic bags are dangerous for sea creatures and how other litter on the beach is dangerous and unhealthy. Talk about how you have just bought some new bins. Point them out and pick up an imaginary plastic bag to put in one of them.
- Ask the children if they can help pick up the rubbish and plastic bags. Hand out some imaginary gloves so they don't get their hands dirty and show them how you want the litter picking up and putting in the bins before letting them help you.
- When the children have finished, ask them to sit down and then turn the sign to '**open.**' Thank the children for their work and go off to get them all some free snacks. Move among the children, inviting them to take some snack food from your imaginary tray. Include foods you know the children will like and consider to be a treat.
- Then take off the item of clothing and narrate your way out of role saying: *'freeze. When the children had finished eating, the café owner went back into the café looking really pleased.'*
- Restart the drama. Remark on what a good job the children have done picking up the litter and saving sea creatures from more plastic.
- Pack your bags and walk away, taking a last look at the sea. Mention the tide has gone out and it is now far away.
- Stop the drama, making it clear that the story has finished.
- Ask the children what they liked doing best in this story about a trip to the sea-side.

> **Reader reflections**
>
> Invite the children to help you find books about the sea-side from those in the classroom. Use the books to read the children stories or information books about the sea-side and the dangers of pollution from plastic and link these to their imaginary experience.

A shorter version:

- Omit the café problem and teacher-in-role. Remark on the litter and plastic bags on the beach as you take part in the activities. Mention the problems litter and plastic bags cause on the beach and ask the children to help you put some in the bins. Buy them food

Figure 4.1 Teacher-in-role rescuing a small creature

from a take away café as a thank you. Put the food containers in the bin after eating the food and end the story there.

A longer version:

- Take an imaginary bus or train ride to the sea-side and back, singing songs to create the idea of travelling.

Extension activities

- Children compose a poster asking people to keep the sea-side clean.
- Children draw and record their favourite sea-side activity along with words to describe it.
- Make a collage of the seaside with hidden pieces of litter for the children to find.
- Use craft materials to design and make models of litter bins for the sea-side.

70　Ages 4-6 (EYFS-Year 1)

EXAMPLE 2: KEEPING THE PARK CLEAN

Suggested Texts:

- *A Day at the Park: Hattie and Friends* by Lesley Berrington
- *Cats' Eye View of Litter* by Octavia Lonergan
- *Charlie's Big Idea: The Adventures of Grandad Wheels* by Brian Abram

Planning and resources

- Select text(s) with specific activities at a park, including any that mention or allude to litter and caring for the environment.

You will need:

- Space to move around freely.
- A small item of clothing to represent a parkkeeper.

What to do

This works in a similar way to the previous seaside example but with the following differences:

- Ask the children to pretend to join you in a story about some children and their teacher who went to visit a park. Talk about what might be in the park and how you might mime the actions. Mention that there may also be things to watch in the park, like skateboarding or ducks in a pond.
- Use the words '*action*' and '*freeze*' to start and stop the drama.
- Start the drama. Using mimed actions, suggesting everyone packs a bag with a ball and another small item to play with on the grass. You can also include a packed lunch.
- Ask them to follow you to some grass in the park where they can play. Sit everyone down and remark on how lovely the park looks with the trees and flowers etc. Then suggest everyone plays with a ball by bouncing or throwing it and catching it. Suggest that it is too dangerous to kick the ball around as it is only a small piece of grass. They can then play with whatever else they have brought.
- After the children have finished playing, ask them to sit down to eat their lunch. Make a point of talking about how important it is not to leave litter from their lunch boxes. Remark on all the overflowing bins you have seen around the park, which means they will have to take their rubbish home.
- Talk about the other activities available in the park, including those mentioned in your chosen text e.g. a skate park as mentioned in **Charlie's Big Idea**.
- Take the children on an imaginary walk to see all the activities. Mime the actions to pretend to go on the swings and a roundabout etc and invite them to join you. Then point out there is a skate board park. Talk about what some of the skate-boarders are wearing,

An imaginary experience 71

and how they are moving up and over the steep parts etc. Then point out the ducks on the pond nearby and suggest they take a look. Accept other things the children might tell you they can see, but make sure this does not take over the focus of the activity. However, if you see a different learning opportunity and are happy to be more open ended you can follow where the children lead.

- Pause the drama. Ask the children to pretend you are someone who works in the park – a park keeper – when you put on the clothing.
- Restart the drama. Introduce the problem of litter in the park by taking on the role of a park keeper who is closing one of the attractions due to the dangerous litter. This could be access to the ducks in the pond or to the animals in a pets corner. Use this role to reflect any comments in the book(s) you are intending to use e.g. **Cats' Eye View of Litter** mentions the dangers of litter for tiny creatures, children, pets and birds.
- In this role, talk about how all the bins are full and then pretend to bring out some new bins from a nearby shed. Show the children how you clear up the litter using gloves and/or spikes and ask them if they would like to help.
- When all the litter has been put in the new bins, thank the children for their work and tell them you can now reopen the attraction.
- Take off the clothing used as a sign of role and pause the drama. Narrate that the park keeper went away feeling really pleased.
- In your former role as the teacher, praise them for their work and then notice a small hedgehog with its head trapped in a plastic cup. Ask the children to be very still and quiet so as not to scare it as you creep towards it. Free the hedgehog and then describe how it runs away.
- Use imaginary hand gel from your bag to clean your hands and then suggest they go to the nearby ice cream van for ice creams. Conclude the drama by eating the ice creams.
- Stop the drama and narrate how the story ended e.g. *'When the children had finished their ice creams they went home feeling very tired but pleased with themselves for helping to keep the park free of litter. And that is the end of the story.'*
- Ask the children what their favourite part of the story was and share yours.
- Read your chosen text(s) and link to the children's imaginary experience as and when appropriate.

Reader reflections

Link the stories and the drama experience to other books about parks and invite the children to compare their imaginary visit with the events in the books.

Extension activity

Children record their visit to the park via art work and/or writing as appropriate. The work can be made into a booklet and added to the other topic books about parks or caring for the environment.

Further suggestions linked to other topics

Farms: A visit to a farm where the farmer is sick and needs help with the farm jobs.

Pets or other animals: A visit to a pet's corner or animal sanctuary where some of the animals have escaped and need retrieving or need living quarters cleaning out.

Weather: A walk on a snowy day where an elderly person needs her path clearing of snow.

Santa: A visit to Santa's workshop, where the elves are sick and need help to finish making and wrapping the toys.

Space: A trip on a space ship to the moon, where the space ship needs repairing before returning.

PART II
Ages 7-11 (Years 2-6)

Figure P.2 Exploring characters' thoughts and feelings
Source: Photograph by www.kerryharrisonphotography.com

Part II focuses on how drama can support reading for meaning when working with children aged 7-11 years (Years 2-6), but some of the activities in Part I, such as the use of puppets, may also be suitable for the youngest children in this age range.

The activities are designed to complement ongoing work on reading comprehension and contribute to reading for pleasure. They are offered as suggested ways of working to be adapted to the context of the school and the particular needs of the children.

DOI: 10.4324/9781003250777-7

5 Frozen depictions

LINKS TO READING FOR MEANING: engaging with texts; inference & deduction; questioning; empathy; characters' thoughts, feelings & relationships; different perspectives; authorial intent; predictions; sequencing; capturing the main idea; making comparisons across texts; exploring key moments themes and concepts; considering the contribution of the illustrator to meaning; retrieving and presenting information; providing justification for opinions on texts; conversations about books.

Rationale

This chapter lists a variety of ways in which freeze-frames can be employed to support reading for meaning. From exploring key moments in a story, to depicting and summarising the main idea in a section of information text, the freeze-frame offers a simple but creative way to investigate a wide range of texts. The discussion involved in creating an authentic version of a moment from a text in a freeze-frame motivates children to interrogate the text. It also creates an opportunity for the teacher to verbalise their own thoughts on how to make inferences and ask questions towards a deeper meaning.

Sculpting has been added to this chapter as another way of depicting the essence of a text through a frozen image.

Contents

Exploring significant moments	76
Recreating and creating images	81
Freeze-frames in sequence	86
The story of an object	88
Read . . . freeze . . . read	90
Predictions, alternatives and comparisons	92
Information texts: depicting the main idea	93
Group sculptures: capturing the essence	94

DOI: 10.4324/9781003250777-8

Drama strategies

Forum theatre
Freeze-frame
Improvisation
Sculpting

Exploring significant moments

In order to make decisions about where the characters in a freeze-frame are looking, what they are thinking and feeling and what the readers and the author might be thinking, the children have to search the text for clues. This requires, amongst other things, a consideration of inference, deduction and authorial intent.

A freeze-frame of a key moment also presents opportunities for adding writing to the frame and/or writing in role as eye witnesses to the moment. Children can also write a caption to summarise what is happening in the freeze-frame.

Some of the following examples focus on creating a freeze-frame via forum theatre, where the whole class direct a small group to produce one freeze-frame. However, once children become confident in creating a freeze-frame as a whole class, they can create and perform their own freeze-frames in small groups, allowing children to express their own interpretations, predictions and speculations about a text.

Planning and resources

- Select a significant moment from a fiction or non-fiction text involving two to four characters.
- Plan alternatives for where each character might be looking and why. For example, in the opening scene from **Goodnight Mister Tom** by **Michelle Magorian** where Mr. Tom reluctantly agrees to host an evacuee you might ask:

   Is William (the evacuee) looking at Tom (his new host)
   because *he is anxious about what might happen?*
   Or is he more likely to be looking at the children he was with on the train ***because*** *he will miss his new friends?*

- In a similar way, prepare two alternatives for what each character might be **thinking** and a general idea about what each character might be **feeling** at that particular moment in the text.

You will need:

- Access to the text extract for each child.
- One A4 heart-shaped outline (Feelings Heart).
- One A4 Thought Bubble outline.
- (Optional) A card displaying the word 'reader' and another card with the name of the author.

- Either an adhesive name tag for each character or a simple costume or item to represent each character.
- (Optional) A device to take a photograph of the freeze-frame during the lesson.

What to do

1 Introduce the freeze-frame

- Give each child access to the text extract.
- Invite the children to act as directors for a freeze-frame depicting a moment in the text.
- Designate a performance area to accommodate the freeze-frame.
- Choose the group of children who will represent the characters.
- Describe the setting for the freeze-frame and indicate the position of any key features e.g. the door to Mr. Tom's house, or the pit the Iron Man has fallen into.

2 Where is everyone looking?

- Ask the first character to stand in the freeze-frame and ask the class where that character is likely to be **looking** and why. Model the process by voicing your suggested alternatives as if you are thinking aloud. Explain any inferences and how you need to use evidence from the text to back up your decision.
- Working in pairs or threes, allow children a few minutes to look for clues in the text to decide where they think that character might be looking. Children in the actual freeze-frame should also take part.
- Consider all feasible responses before asking the child representing the character to select the final version. Make it clear that this freeze-frame is just one interpretation and that there could be other equally valid perspectives, as long as they are backed up by textual evidence.
- Use the same process with the other characters to select an appropriate orientation for each.
- Make a **draft freeze-frame** to show the agreed positions of the characters.

    It's useful to describe the moment and do a countdown of '1-2-3-freeze . . . Hold it . . . 1-2-3-relax.'

- (Optional) Take a photo of the freeze-frame and share it with the children who are playing the characters, so they can see the effect.

3 Thought Bubbles

- Make another draft freeze-frame and hold the Thought Bubble over each character's head in turn, asking the class what that character might be **thinking**. Ask the children to suggest two alternative thoughts for each character based on what they know of the text, before offering your own suggestions. Encourage thoughts that are more than a couple of words.
- The child playing the character should select a thought from the suggestions to speak aloud during the freeze-frame.

Ages 7–11 (Years 2–6)

- Alternatively choose another group of children to speak out the characters' thoughts during the freeze-frame.
- Decide on an order for speaking the thoughts for the next freeze-frame. Tell the class the words you will use to introduce the thoughts, so the first character knows when to speak and tell them how you will end it e.g. *'1-2-3-freeze . . . this is what the characters might have been thinking . . . 1-2-3-relax.'*
- Another way of presenting thoughts is for individual characters to step out of the freeze-frame to tell everyone what they're thinking at that moment.

4 Feelings Hearts

- To open up a discussion on how each character might be **feeling,** as opposed to *thinking*, hold the heart-shaped outline (Feelings Heart) over each character in turn to collect appropriate feelings, asking the question *How do you know?* To keep up the pace of the lesson, invite suggestions from the class instead of allowing time for groups, but insist on evidence from the text.
- (Optional) Link the feelings to icons showing different emotions e.g. a smiley face, a disappointed face etc. Draw these on cards for children to hold above the character's heads before or during the freeze-frame. You may have more than one icon on each card if there are several emotions.
- Ask the class to advise the characters on how best to show what they are feeling in the freeze-frame through expressions and body language.
- Make a **final freeze-frame** with the appropriate expressions and spoken thoughts.
- Work with the class to write a caption summarising what is happening in the freeze-frame.

Further options

5 Reader card

- Hold the reader card above each character's head and ask the children the following two questions: *'What do you, as readers, feel about this character?' 'What has the author written to make you feel the way you do about this character?'*
- Challenge the class to change some of the author's words in the text to see if that would change the way they perceive the character e.g. change the words used to describe a threatening character so they seem less threatening and vice versa.

6 Author card

- Give a child the author card with the name of the author written on. Ask the class to consider how the author has portrayed each character up to this point in the text.
- Go through each character in turn. If the child with the author card thinks the author wants the reader to like that character, they should stand next to that character. If they think the author wants the reader to dislike the character they should stand away from the character at the edge of the freeze-frame. If they feel the author is indifferent they should stand at a mid-point or remain seated holding the card.

- Ask the class to do thumbs up or down if they agree/disagree with these choices and ask them why. Encourage evidence from the text. Alternatively, use the author card yourself and ask the class if they agree or disagree with your choices.
- Develop this into a discussion about how writers use language to influence what their readers feel about the characters and suggest they can employ similar techniques in their own writing.

7 Writing in the frame

- Adapt the following to the context of your freeze-frame:

    Somewhere in the frame there is some writing. It may be on a paper folded up in someone's pocket, it may be displayed on a wall or building, it may be on a table or chair or even on the ground. What might it be? A note, diary, calendar, letter, list?

- After collecting a couple of suggestions, children work in pairs to decide what that piece of writing might be and where it might be located in the freeze-frame. They should then compose the first couple of lines.
- Remake the freeze-frame with the characters standing in their places but not frozen.
- Ask each pair to state where their paper would be located, before asking one of them to place it in the frame as near as possible to where it would be located.
- After asking the characters to re make the freeze-frame, walk into the frame and read out the papers one at a time.
- Ask the children to finish off their piece of writing and/or select one for the whole class to complete.

Reader reflections

Ask children if they would like to see more Thought Bubbles on illustrations in novels. Would they be appropriate for all novels?

Link to graphic novels where stories are told in images with bubbles for thoughts, sounds and speech such as **Roller Girl by Victoria Jamieson.**

Extension activities

Children write in role as eye witnesses to the moment depicted in the freeze-frame e.g. bystanders, neighbours, news reporters or even nearby objects.

EXAMPLE 1: A NOVEL

Text: *The Iron Man* by Ted Hughes

80   *Ages 7-11 (Years 2-6)*

Planning and resources

- Children need to be familiar with the story up to the end of Chapter 2 and need sight of the last few pages during the activity.

You will need:

- One Thought Bubble and one Feelings Heart.
- A performance space.
- A chair to represent the pit.
- Adhesive name labels or simple costumes for Hogarth, the Iron Man and two farmers.

What to do

- Focus on the moment when the Iron Man has fallen in the pit dug by the farmers. Use the line from the text *'Only Hogarth felt suddenly sorry'* as a caption.
- Choose one child to represent Hogarth, one to represent the Iron Man and two other children to represent the farmers.
- Place a chair in the centre of the frame. The Iron Man sits on this as if he is inside the pit.
- Ask where each character might be looking, given what we know of the text, e.g.: *'Is Hogarth looking at the Iron Man because he feels guilty for tricking him, is he looking away because he can't face him or is he looking somewhere else?'*
- Continue with the Thought Bubble, Feelings Heart and reader and author cards as appropriate.
- Writing in the frame could include notes in the pockets of the characters.

> ### Extension activity
>
> Children write eye witness accounts of the incident in role as other farmers, neighbours or a journalist who was there at the time.

EXAMPLE 2: SHAKESPEARE'S MACBETH ACT 1 SCENE 1 THE WITCHES SCENE

Texts:

- *Macbeth* **by William Shakespeare**
- *Comic Book Shakespeare Macbeth* **by Simon Greaves**
- *Mr. William Shakespeare's Plays* **by Marcia Williams**

Planning, resources and what to do

Make the freeze-frames as in the overview, with the following adaptations:

- Children need to be familiar with the scene and have sight of it during the activity.
- You will need a Feelings Heart and a Thought Bubble.
- Create a freeze-frame of the moment at the end of the scene when *All* the witches chant the lines as they are about to leave to meet with Macbeth.
- Use a Feelings Heart and a Thought Bubble to ask questions such as *'What are the witches thinking and feeling?'*
- Ask: *'Why has Shakespeare chosen to start the play with the witches? Why has he chosen to end the scene with these two lines?'*
- Look at how comic or graphic novel versions depict this scene in different ways and compare to the more realistic depiction in this freeze-frame.
- Invite children to write their own comic version of this scene, with key lines from the text and Thought Bubbles.

Reader reflections

Ask the children to consider how we feel about witches today compared to the past. Link to novels that mention the persecution of witches such as **The Somerset Tsunami** by **Emma Carroll** set in 1616 and **A Kind of Spark** by **Elle McNicoll** set in modern times.

Extension activities

- Let children create a short soundscape to accompany this freeze-frame, adding key words from the text to help create the mood. You can pre-record the soundscape, adding the words when the freeze-frame is performed.
- Show an animated version of this opening scene followed by a live theatre or film version. Compare with each other and with the comic versions. Use this to illustrate how the same scene can be interpreted and expressed in different ways.

Recreating and creating images

Photographs of historical and more recent real-life events found in information books can form the basis of a freeze-frame. For example, the photograph of the moment when Howard Carter discovered the tomb of Tutankhamun or a photograph of evacuees in the Second World War.

Illustrations and paintings found in picture books, stories, poetry books and information books can also be explored via a freeze-frame. This can be a recreation based on a version of one specific illustration or created using several illustrations from one or more texts on a similar topic.

Information books about artists like L. S. Lowry who paint scenes with people in them, often contain copies of the paintings which can be recreated via freeze-frames. This creates a personal relationship with a painting which helps motivate children to read more information texts about the artist and the painting.

Poems like haiku are often accompanied by paintings and other illustrations, where their link to the poem can be explored via a freeze-frame of the illustration.

Children can explore their own ideas for illustrations in a text through creating freeze-frames. This simple method opens up a valuable debate on the contribution illustrators make to the meaning of a text. It also re-enforces the idea that, whilst an illustration is one person's interpretation of the text, other interpretations are equally valid providing they remain true to the text.

Proceed as in the section on 'exploring significant moments' using the following Examples as models:

EXAMPLE 1: A REAL LIFE EVENT – THE GREAT FIRE OF LONDON

Texts:

- ***Vlad and the Great Fire of London* by Kate and Sam Cunningham**
- ***The Great Fire of London: Anniversary Edition* by Emma Adams**

Planning and resources

- Select an illustration from your chosen text as a basis for a freeze-frame or use illustrations from more than one text to create an imaginary version of the event e.g. the day after the fire when a group of people are looking at the damage. The people in this freeze-frame could include real characters such as Samuel Pepys and/or King Charles. You can also invent characters to represent ordinary people like someone whose shop was lost, a child who escaped by swimming the river or imaginary eye witnesses from a story like Vlad the flea and Boxton the rat in ***Vlad and the Great Fire of London***.
- Children will need access to the text(s) for reference.

You will need:

- Adhesive name labels for each character and/or simple costumes.
- A Thought Bubble and a Feelings Heart.

What to do

- Select a group of children to represent the characters in the freeze-frame.
- Select a point in the room to represent the direction of the fire.
- Make the freeze-frame using the Thought Bubble and Feelings Heart to deepen the meaning, referring to the text(s) for evidence and information when required.

Reader reflections

Invite children to compare the story version of the Great Fire of London with the information book on the same topic. Look at other examples of books on historical topics and ask children if they have any preference for a story or an information book when learning about real events.

Talk about the benefits of reading both kinds of books.

Extension activities

- Children sketch the moment represented by the freeze-frame as if it were in a newspaper. They write a heading above and sentences underneath to describe what is happening.
- Children write a diary extract in role as one of the observers in the frame, which can be linked to reading about Samuel Pepys' diary.

EXAMPLE 2: HAIKU

Text: *Icy Morning Haiku* from *Weird, Wild and Wonderful* by James Carter and Neal Layton

Planning and resources

- Children need sight of the poem and accompanying illustration during the activity and an idea of what a haiku is.

You will need:

- A Thought bubble and a Feelings Heart.
- A small performance area and a chair.
- Adhesive name labels for the three creatures in the poem.

84 Ages 7-11 (Years 2-6)

What to do

- Read the poem and show the children the illustration on the facing page.
- Explain the freeze-frame strategy and invite the children to be directors to create their own version of this illustration.
- Select three children to represent the creatures in the frame, using the adhesive labels to identify them.
- Place a chair in the centre for ground level. Ask the Cat to stand up to represent the tree level and use the floor to represent under the water.
- Use the Feelings Heart to initiate a discussion about how each character might be feeling. Then use the Thought Bubble to ask the class what each character might be thinking based on what can be inferred from the poem and illustration. Ask the characters to make the final decisions after listening to the suggestions from the class.
- Make the freeze-frame with the characters speaking out their thoughts in turn or with other children standing behind the characters to voice the thoughts.
- Talk about what might happen next and make another freeze-frame to depict the prediction, along with speaking thoughts.
- Ask children if they feel the illustration of the poem would benefit from adding Thought Bubbles as in their freeze-frame and what they feel the illustration adds to the reading of the poem.

Reader reflections

Explore and compare how haiku are illustrated in other books such as:

My First Book of Haiku Poems by Esperanza Ramirez-Christensen
Polka Dot Poems: 100 Weird and Wonderful Nature Haiku by Zaro Weil
Earth Verse: Haiku from the Ground Up by Sam M. Walker.

Use agree/disagree cards for the '**where do you stand now?**' strategy to explore children's opinions on the following statements:

All haiku in children's books should be illustrated.
A good haiku presents an image in words and does not need an illustration.

Extension activities

Children write their own haiku in role as another creature who witnessed what happened next.
Support the reading and writing of haiku with books such as **Write Your Own Haiku for Kids** by Patricia Donegan.

EXAMPLE 3: *BY ASH, OAK AND THORN* BY MELISSA HARRISON

Optional text: *Window* by Jeannie Baker

Planning and resources

- All children need half an A4 sheet of plain paper and a pencil.
- Children need sight of the first section of the book entitled ASH.

You will need:

- One Feelings Heart.
- A performance space.

What to do

- Read the children the first section of the book entitled **Ash** and point out that there are few illustrations up to this point, apart from the cover and a map. Ask them why they think the author might have made this decision and talk about how she uses words effectively to paint pictures in a reader's imagination.
- Read the section in Chapter 4 describing the camp. Then read it again, asking the children to do a quick sketch of what they see in their imagination as they listen. Emphasise this is meant to be very fast, like taking notes rather than a finished drawing and stress that there are no right or wrong ways to picture this, as long as it fits with the text.
- Allow children a few minutes after the reading to finish their sketches, then ask them to form small groups to compare their sketches. Ask groups to report back on something they all included and something that was different about their sketches.
- Use this as an opportunity to re-enforce the idea that whilst there are similarities due to the descriptions in the story, all readers have a slightly different response and form different pictures in their minds. Talk about how this difference often depends on a reader's own experience. For example, if a reader has been camping they might have a better understanding of some of the words and form a different picture in their mind than someone who hasn't been camping.
- Ask the children what moment they would choose to illustrate this part of the story.
- Select one of their suggestions that could be represented as a freeze-frame.
- Make the freeze-frame using a Feelings Heart to help characters create appropriate expressions. Omit the Thought Bubble unless children feel that thoughts should be included in the illustration.
- Ask the children to suggest a title for their illustration from the text.
- Make the freeze-frame again, asking a child to read out the caption at the start.
- Ask what this illustration would add to the story if it were included. Use this to talk about the function of illustrations as contributors to the meaning of a story.

- Talk about the importance of illustrations in picture books, especially where the pictures tell the whole story. Compare how a theme in this book about changes in nature and the environment over time is handled differently in a picture book like **Window** by **Jeannie Baker** or information books about changes in nature.
- (Optional) Repeat the activity after reading *Oak and Thorn*, asking children to work in small groups to create and then share freeze-frames based on their own ideas for illustrations.

Reader reflections

Use 'yes' and 'no' cards for a '**where do you stand now?**' activity to stimulate discussion on the role of illustrations using the following type of questions:

'Should every children's story have illustrations?'
'Do you prefer story books without illustrations, so you can imagine what is happening yourself?'
'Should illustrations always include the characters?'
'Do information books always need illustrations?'

Extension activities

Give children an opportunity to browse through a small sample of books to compare and review the illustrations in terms of adding interest and helping readers understand the meaning. Provide a mixture of fiction and non-fiction and ask them to consider the different kinds of illustrations in an information book compared to fiction.

Freeze-frames in sequence

Arranging a number of freeze-frames in a sequence is the drama equivalent of a storyboard. Make each freeze-frame as in the section on *Exploring Significant Moments*.

What to do

- Working as a whole class, make three freeze-frames to represent the beginning, middle and end of a story or real-life event.
- The freeze-frames should be accompanied by appropriate captions, either from the text or composed by the children.

EXAMPLE: ERNEST SHACKLETON'S JOURNEY

Text: *Shackleton's Journey* by William Grill

Planning and resources

- Children will need access to the parts of text relating to three selected key moments representing a sequence of all or some of the events.

You will need:

- A performance area at the front of the class.
- A Thought Bubble.
- An adhesive label for each character.
- A Feelings Heart, a reader card and an author card as appropriate.

What to do

- Explain that the following key moments from the story will be represented in three freeze-frames:

    1. The moment when Shackleton set off on his adventure.
    2. The moment Shackleton and his crew watched their ship The Endurance break up and sink beneath the ice.
    3. The moment the remaining survivors of the Ross Sea party were rescued or the moment when everyone returned home.

- Use a Thought Bubble, a Feelings Heart and 'writing in the frame' for all three freeze-frames, with reference to the information in the text.
- Compare and contrast the thoughts and feelings in the freeze-frames.
- Use the reader and author cards to explore how the information has been presented.

Reader reflections

Ask:

- 'Do you prefer to read about real life adventures via information books or stories?'
- 'Do they tell the story differently? If so how do they differ?'

Link to books that tell fictionalised versions of real-life stories such as **Arctic Star by Tom Palmer** and **Street Child by Berlie Doherty.**

> **Extension activities**
> - Sketch the freeze-frame of when they first set sail, as if in a newspaper of the time, with a headline and accompanying short article.
> - Write a diary entry by one of the crew about the loss of the *Endurance*.

Further Suggestions

Everest: The Remarkable Story of Edmund Hillary and Tenzing Norgay by Alexandra Stewart

Select three key moments from this story to depict in freeze-frames.

The story of an object

Many authors include significant objects as extended metaphors, to reflect the development of the protagonist or the arc of the story. These objects arrive in the story with a history that is often hinted at but not fully explored. Freeze-frames provide a way for children to create and express not only their own version of the back story, but how an author invests the object with significance and then threads it through the narrative to reflect key moments of tension and resolution. For example, a significant object in **Angel's Child by Larraine S Harrison** is a jewellery box belonging to 12-year-old Amber's late Granny. Amber's own sketch of the box appears as the first illustration in Chapter 1. The story of this box is a metaphor for Amber's struggle as she attempts to help a neglected little girl and cope with the impact of her grandad's dementia. It also represents changes in her co-protagonist Emil and other events in the story.

What to do

Use the following example as a model for defining and discussing significant objects in other stories:

EXAMPLE: JEWELLERY BOX

Text: *Angel's Child* by Larraine S Harrison

Planning and resources

- Children should be familiar with the story before the activity.
- Children need sight of the illustration of the box at the start of Chapter 1.

Figure 5.1 Amber's sketch-book in *Angel's Child* by Larraine S. Harrison

You will need

- Copies of the following four text extracts, one for each group:

1   Chapter 1:

'Where's Granny's jewellery box? It used to be on that shelf.'
'I've given it to Katrin.'
'But Granny's father gave it to her. She used to keep her rings in it. We all loved it.'
'Well Katrin loved it too.'
'I thought you promised it to Mum.'

2   Chapter 10:

She reached out her hand and grasped the box. Whatever happened now, she would face the consequences, but Granny's box was not going to be sold.

3   Chapter 13:

She took Granny's box out of the drawer and unwrapped it, tracing her fingers over the leaves and flowers across the lid. She had a lump in her throat thinking about losing it, but she had to take it back.

4   Chapter 17:

> There was a pause before Dave opened the lounge door.
> 'I've got it,' he said.
> As her hands reached out for the precious jewellery box, she felt as if her Granny was smiling at her.
> 'Thank you so much,' she whispered.

You will need:

- Enough space for small groups to practise and share their freeze-frames.

What to do

- Show the illustration of the box on the first page of Chapter 1, which is a sketch drawn by Amber in her sketch-book. Ask the children why this is placed at the start of the book and what this tells the reader. Remind them that Amber drew the box from memory after her Grandad had given it away. Ask the children what this tells the reader about the past and how she feels about the box.
- Using the section 'Exploring significant moments' as a model, work with the class to create a speculative flash back freeze-frame of the moment when Granny's father gave her the jewellery box. They should also decide on a suitable caption. Use a Thought bubble and Feelings Heart to explore the thoughts and emotions.
- Arrange the children into small groups and allocate a text extract to each group. In larger classes some groups will have the same extract.
- Ask each group to prepare a freeze-frame to illustrate their text extract. They should include a caption and speaking thoughts when they share it with the class. They should also be prepared to answer questions about their interpretation.
- Show the freeze-frames in sequence, so they tell the story of the box.
- Ask the children if they think the story of the box is similar to any other aspects of the story, such as what happened to the characters or the events. Use this as an opportunity to talk about extended metaphors and authorial intent.
- Consider other aspects of this story that could have a similar function. Draw the children's attention to the mention of food threaded through the book i.e. from a lack of food at the beginning to enjoying a special cake at the end and the fact that Emil wants to be a chef when he grows up. Talk about what food might represent in terms of the story.

Read . . . freeze . . . read

This activity involves the teacher freezing key moments during reading aloud, to create an opportunity for children to focus on what is happening. This sharpens children's listening skills and encourages different perspectives and visualisations of key moments in the text. There are two versions of this activity; one encourages a reader response, whilst the other involves spontaneous group depictions of the moment via freeze-frames.

Planning, resources and what to do

- Choose a suitable text to read aloud.

Version 1: individual reader responses

- Make one Feelings Heart.
- Working as a class, collect and display some words or phrases inside a heart-shaped outline that describe how a reader might feel when reading a story e.g. interested, scared, bored, feeling sorry for a character, disliking a character, confused, puzzled, nervous etc. Alternatively draw icons to represent these feelings.
- Start to read the extract and call '*freeze*' to pause at a key point in the story.
- Ask all children to consider what they are feeling as readers at this point. If you are using icons, they can write these down. Then pass the Feelings Heart to some children, asking them to share what they are feeling and why. This can be verbal or by drawing an appropriate icon and holding it up with a verbal explanation. Ask others to give a thumbs up or down to agree or disagree each time and invite discussion.
- Read more of the extract and repeat the activity at another point using the Feelings Heart.

Version 2: Group responses

The version involves the teacher reading the text aloud and stopping at various points for children to make freeze-frames of that particular moment. These freeze-frames are potentially broader in scope, allowing children to use their bodies to include a representation of inanimate objects if appropriate. There is a time limit for making the freeze-frames which demands a rapid but creative first response, which is later explored. Children need to be confident with making group freeze-frames for this activity.

Planning and resources

- If you have a child who may find rapid responses disturbing, talk to them about the activity beforehand and/or include them in a different way, such as asking them to help you observe the freeze-frames or be the time keeper.

You will need

- Space for groups to make their freeze-frames close to where they are sitting.
- One Thought Bubble.

What to do

- Arrange the children to sit in small groups.
- Read the story aloud stopping at one or two key moments to say *freeze-frame*. This is the signal for groups to make a quick freeze-frame of the moment you have just described.

Depending on the text and your objectives you can allow children to include representations of inanimate objects in these freeze-frames, such as objects, buildings or natural features.
- Give a time limit to encourage children to make a spontaneous response. The exact amount of time will depend on the children, but it's helpful to do a countdown for the last ten or 15 seconds, before stopping the activity.
- Ask groups to share their freeze-frames one at a time. Make a brief but positive comment about each of the freeze-frames, before asking one or two children in each group to say who or what they represent and/or hold the Thought Bubble over them to share their thoughts.
- Read more of the text and repeat with another key moment.

Predictions, alternatives and comparisons

What to do

Proceed as in the section 'Exploring significant moments,' with the following adaptations:

- Working as a whole class or in groups, pause the reading of a text to allow children to create a freeze-frame showing a prediction of what might happen next. You can also use a freeze-frame to speculate about what might happen to the characters after the story has finished.
- If children are working in groups, they should add a caption and decide who will read this out when sharing.
- If you are working as a whole class, make two or three different predictions and compare them in terms of their potential to move the story forward.
- If you are reading information texts about changes in landscape or historical changes, make two freeze-frames to depict them side by side to make comparisons e.g. 'then' and 'now' for changes over time or differences in everyday life in a village scene compared with in a town. Link with texts showing change over time such as **Window by Jeannie Baker.**
- Look at two or three different versions of a story such as a fairy tale and create freeze-frames of the key differences alongside each other, to compare what the characters might be thinking and feeling in each version.

EXAMPLE: COMPARING A FAIRY TALE

Texts:

- ***The Little Mermaid* by Hans Christian Andersen**
- ***Nen and the Lonely Fisherman* by Ian Eagleton and James Mayhew**

What to do

- Discuss the similarities and differences between these two versions and work as a class to select one or two main differences on which to base two contrasting freeze-frames.
- Talk about the possible thoughts and feelings of the characters in each freeze-frame and compare them.

- Link with texts that tell alternative, amusing or different kinds of fairy tales such as:

    Gender Swapped Fairy Tales by **Karrie Fransman and Jonathan Plackett**
    Forgotten Fairy Tales of Brave and Brilliant Girls by **Susanna Davidson et al.**
    Who's Afraid of the Big Bad Book? by **Lauren Child**
    Spot the Fairy Tales (Ten Tiny Senryu) by **James Carter** (from *Weird, Wild and Wonderful*)
    Red Riding Hood and the Sweet Little Wolf by **Rachael Mortimer** (N.B. This is a book for younger children but relevant here due to the way the wolf is portrayed.)

- After sharing some suggestions, invite the children to work in groups to create their own freeze-frames showing an alternative beginning for another fairy tale and then share them with the rest of the class along with a caption.

Information texts: depicting the main idea

This activity invites groups of children to use their bodies in a freeze-frame to portray an abstract concept or depict the main idea from an information text. They then bring the freeze-frame to life for a few seconds to add movement before freezing it again. They may also use more than one freeze-frame to represent a sequence. Margaret Branscombe's work in ***Teaching through Embodied Learning*** (2019, Routledge) reveals how creating tableau (freeze-frames) based on scientific concepts or geographical phenomena can motivate children to read the information texts carefully. She also found that using their bodies to express that meaning facilitated a deeper level of understanding.

Planning and resources

- This works best when children are confident with the idea of making freeze-frames in small groups.
- Children need access to information text(s) and other texts relating to your chosen topic. For example an information text such as **Forces and Magnets** by **Peter Riley** links well with the poem **Magnetic Me** by **Neal Zetter.**
- Select a short extract from the information text(s) for each group to depict in their freeze-frame. Groups can be given the same extract or different extracts, as appropriate.

You will need:

- A copy of the relevant text(s) for each child or group.
- Enough space for groups to practise and perform their freeze-frames.
- (Optional) One or two props made available to each group for their final freeze-frames.
- Writing materials for each group to record the main idea in their text extract.

What to do

- Arrange the children into groups of three or four.
- Give each group a short extract of information text along with a copy of any supporting texts such as a poem, news report or story extract. Provide access to any relevant background information or further explanations about the topic.

- Ask each group to write down the main idea of their extract in just a few sentences.
- If the main idea has potential for movement like magnetism, ask groups to bring their freeze-frame to life for a few seconds to express that movement, before ending with a second freeze-frame.
- Give groups a time limit but be prepared to be flexible. When one or two groups have finished, give a countdown of a minute or so for the others.
- Ask each group to read out their sentences and identify who or what they are representing in the freeze-frame, before sharing with the rest of the class.
- Discuss links with any supporting text e.g. how the poem *Magnetic Me* expresses magnetism in a different way to the information texts.

A Simplified Version

- Read the text extract(s) as a whole class and work with the children to produce one freeze-frame that can be brought to life and frozen again if appropriate.

Group sculptures: capturing the essence

This activity facilitates the exploration of meaning in a text by using the body in a more symbolic way to express thinking and feeling. It seeks to embody the essence of a text, requiring a level of reflection and understanding that moves beyond the literal interpretation of events. It can be applied to themes or a simple story.

Use the following example and further suggestions as models:

EXAMPLE: KINDNESS AND CRUELTY

Suggested Texts:

- *The Snow Queen by Hans Christian Anderson*: P. J. Lynch
- *It's . . . Kindness* by James Carter from *Weird, Wild and Wonderful*
- *Ugly Sister Sonnet* by Sue Hardy Dawson from *Where Zebras Go.*
- *Holes* by Louis Sacher

Planning and resources

- Select a text which contains clear examples of kindness and cruelty.
- Children should be familiar with the chosen text prior to the activity.

You will need

- A cleared space for children to make the sculptures.
- Cards and pens to write titles for the sculptures.

What to do

Introduction: the art gallery

- *Sculptures:* Write the word 'kindness' on a card and ask the children to imagine this was the title of a sculpture in an art gallery or in a public place.
- Ask the children to stand in a circle facing outwards. Tell them that when you say the words *'Turn and freeze'* – they should turn into the centre of the circle and freeze as if they were the figures in the sculpture entitled *Kindness*. Give children time to think about how they will portray Kindness with their bodies before they turn around to make the sculpture. They may need some suggestions if they are new to this way of working e.g. ask for examples of acts of kindness in everyday life and talk about how they could be represented like giving a drink to someone, stooping to help pick up spilt shopping, putting an arm round someone to comfort them etc.
- When they are ready, ask the children to turn to the centre and freeze to make a group sculpture entitled *Kindness*. Walk round the sculpture and comment positively but speculatively on it before asking the children to relax.
- Talk about the images in the sculpture and what kind of positions and facial expressions were made
- Then repeat the process with another sculpture entitled *Cruelty* and invite comparisons.

Link to the text(s)

- Hold up your chosen text and make the statement: *'I wonder how our sculptures link with this text.'* Discuss possible links.

Group Sculptures

- Collect some specific examples of kindness in your chosen text.
- Organise the class into groups of four. Ask two children to be A and two to be B.
- All the As in the class stand side by side in a large circle facing inwards. Then the Bs stand facing their A partners, to make an inner circle. Explain that A children are the sculptors and B children are the clay. This inner circle of B children will represent the first sculpture.
- Ask the As to make their Bs into a sculpture indicating *Kindness* **as reflected in the text**, by asking them to direct their bodies into certain positions. No touching is allowed but As can model how they want Bs to look. They should stand back when they have completed the sculpture and/or give a time limit.
- Make it clear that each individual sculpture will form part of a whole group sculpture based on kindness as evidenced in the text.
- When they have made their sculptures ask all the Bs to hold their positions in a freeze, whilst all the As walk around the sculpture to look at all the group sculpture. Discuss the different interpretations of kindness as the As walk round.

- Collect some specific examples of cruelty in the text.
- Now repeat the activity with Bs making As into a sculpture entitled *Cruelty* as reflected in the text and then talk about the differences between the two sculptures. Children may need to be reminded of the *Kindness* sculpture before comparing the two.

Further Suggestions

- Create sculptures based on texts with incidents of **friendship** and **falling out** such as:

  The Shark Caller by Zillah Bethell
  The Middler by Kirsty Applebaum
  School Coach Trip: A Poem by Coral Rumble
  Little Light: A Verse Novel by Coral Rumble
  Fearless: A Graphic Novel by Kenny Porter and Zac Wilcox

- Create sculptures entitled **Friends** and **Enemies** based on texts where friendships are forged in the fight against a common foe such as:

  Orphans of the Tide by Straun Murray
  Nevertell by Katharine Orton

Reference

Branscombe. M. (2019) TEACHING THROUGH EMBODIED LEARNING: Dramatizing Key Concepts from Informational Texts. Routledge

6 Actions and performances

LINKS TO READING FOR MEANING: engaging with texts; dramatising stories; empathy; sequencing; summarising plots; extending vocabulary; preparing and learning texts to read with expression; figurative language; comparing different poems on the same theme.

Rationale

Re-enacting and performing a range of texts in a variety of ways helps children explore the different ways in which those texts convey meaning e.g. performing a version of a novel in the form of a play or reciting different types of poems on the same theme.

The need to find appropriate actions to represent words and phrases also extends vocabulary and provides an opportunity to explore how the meaning of words depends on their context e.g. words used in figurative language. An added bonus is the increased attention children pay to a text, when they know they will be asked to perform it.

Contents

Action freeze narration	98
The silent movie	100
Actions for words and phrases	103
Choral reading with actions	109
Performing poems on a similar theme	110
Performing riddles	111
Improvisations	113
On air	115
Performing and presenting playscripts	118

Drama strategies

Action/freeze narration
Actions
Character circle

DOI: 10.4324/9781003250777-9

Echo
Freeze
Improvisations
Playscripts
Role-on-the-wall
Silent movie
Teacher-in-role
Where do you stand now? Spiders web

Action freeze narration

Action Freeze Narration allows all the children in a class to re-enact short extracts from stories. It works best with children in Years 2-4.

Planning and resources

- Select a story the children are familiar with and choose a few short extracts with potential for mimed actions. The extracts can be from different sections of the story as long as they follow the same sequence as the book. For example in the story of **The Iron Man by Ted Hughes** you might use the following three extracts:

    1   From the beginning of Chapter 2 to when Hogarth tells his dad he has seen the Iron Man.
    2   From further on in Chapter 2: *'Next morning the farmers were shouting with anger'* up to *'the hole looked like a freshly ploughed field.'*
    3   Chapter 3: from *'Eat all you can'* to the end of the chapter.

- Summarise the main events in the extracts in your own words and/or words from the text.

You will need:

- A hall or cleared classroom space.

What to do

Introduction

- Share an outline of your chosen text extracts with the children and explain how they will be asked to perform mimed actions as you narrate the extracts.
- If you are in a large space, ask the children to find a space on their own. If you are in a cleared classroom, designate each child a space to perform their actions.
- When you say *action*, the children should walk around without making contact with anyone else (or walk on the spot if in a defined space) and then stop in a frozen position when you say *'freeze.'* They should hold the freeze until you say *Relax*.

Actions and performances 99

- Choose a character from the first extract and explain that everyone will play this character at the same time using mimed actions.
- Explain how you will use the words *'action'* and *'freeze'* to start and stop.
- Make it clear at what point in the extract the activity will start and when it will finish e.g. *'The first part of our action/freeze story begins at Chapter 2 when Hogarth was fishing in a stream and finishes when he reaches home, telling his dad he has seen an Iron Man.'*
- Ask the children how the character might be feeling at different points in the extract and ask for suggestions and demonstrations on how these feelings and events could be expressed through the mimed actions e.g. feeling scared when spotting the Iron Man, feeling anxious when running home and arriving gasping for breath.
- Agree a frozen position to start and another one to finish on.
- Emphasise the need for the children to listen carefully to the reading, so they know what actions to perform and when.

Rehearsal

- On the word *'action,'* read the first extract as the children mime the actions. Then freeze it after the last sentence and ask them to relax.
- Point out any imaginative or effective mimed actions indicating the feelings of the character and any interesting frozen positions and ask the children responsible to recreate them to show the others.
- Repeat the action freeze narration with other extracts where the children might need to play a different character.

Performing the sequence

- All the extracts can now be repeated without the intervening discussions, so children gain confidence and a sense of the sequence of the events.

Reflecting on the activity

- Ask children which parts they enjoyed acting out the most and which parts worked the best with actions.

Reader reflections

Ask:

- *'Did enacting this part of the story help you understand it better? If so in what ways?'*
- *'Do you prefer to see a story enacted in a play, a dance or a film or would you rather read the story in a book and why?'*

The silent movie

This activity works best with Years 4-6 but can be simplified for younger children.

Planning and resources

- Divide the text into a series of very short scenes, based on key actions or events in the main plot.
- Write a summary of each scene in as few words as possible, focusing on the actions rather than feelings and details.

You will need:

- An adhesive name label for each character.
- A cleared performance space for a small group.
- Small props or costumes as appropriate.

What to do

Introduction

- Explain the purpose of the silent movie activity as a brisk overview of the plot, but stress that the movements themselves will not be artificially speeded up.
- Make it clear that the performers will be walking through and miming the main actions, as you narrate each scene.
- Allocate character roles to some of the children and ask them to wear the labels. Make sure these children are comfortable with performing to an audience.
- The rest of the class are to be directors as well as an audience, making suggestions and prompting the entrances.

The Rehearsal

- Read out the first scene and ask the class to suggest potential mimed actions for the characters. Then narrate that scene as the characters walk through and mime the actions.
- Repeat the previous activity with the subsequent scenes.
- This first attempt will not be perfect and is meant to be light hearted, so try to plough through without too much stopping and starting.

The Performance

- Iron out any problems that occurred during the rehearsal and run the silent movie again, without the intervening discussion, so it runs smoothly. A confident child or children from the class may contribute to the narration of the final performance.
- Perform in assembly or record on video if appropriate.

> **Reader reflections**
>
> Ask:
>
> - 'Do you prefer to read stories with straightforward plots or ones with twists and turns and why?'
> - 'Can anyone name a favourite book they have read that has a good plot and say why they liked it?'

Extension activity

Children write silent movie scenes for other versions of the same text or parts of other texts.

EXAMPLE: THESEUS AND THE MINOTAUR

Texts:

- **Greek Myths** by Marcia Williams
- **The Orchard Book of Greek Myths** by Geraldine McCaughrean

What to do

- Introduce the activity as previously described.
- Carry out a Silent Movie version of part or the whole story in a similar manner to the following illustration:

Theseus and the minotaur

Scene 1
Characters:
King Minos
The King of Athens
Narration
'King Minos of Crete was unhappy. The Minotaur who lived in a labyrinth on Crete, was eating his young people. So he made a deal with the King of Athens.
'I will not attack Athens for 9 years,' he said, 'if you will send a boat of young people from Athens to be fed to the Minotaur when the 9 years are up.' The king of Athens had no navy to defend himself, so he agreed.'

(All leave the stage.)
Suggestions for mimed actions:
King Minos shakes his head and/or wipes his eyes in sadness.
The King of Athens arrives and shakes hands with King Minos.

Scene 2
Characters:
The King of Athens
Two children to represent the young people
Theseus
Narration
'After 9 years the King of Athens chose some young people to be fed to the Minotaur. The King's young son Prince Theseus said he would go with them and kill the Minotaur. His father begged him not to go but he wouldn't listen and left with the young people.'
(All leave the stage.)
Suggestions for mimed actions:

> The King points to the young people, who look scared.
> Theseus steps forward and flexes his muscles as the young people look surprised.
> The King falls on one knee to beg Theseus not to go.
> The King looks sad as they all wave goodbye and leave.

- Adapt the sections and mimed actions to suit whatever version you have chosen.
- Repeat the Silent Movie at least once more, so children develop a good sense of the plot and the characters become more confident with anticipating when to take part.

Extension activities

- Give children another part or another version of the story of Theseus and the Minotaur and ask them to write it as a silent movie.
- Give children another Greek myth and invite them to write part of it as a silent movie.

Reader reflections

- Show children an animated version and invite them to compare this to the written version in terms of reader/audience interest and the amount of detail they cover.
- Invite children to talk about other film, dance or play versions of stories they have read and how they compare. Include a discussion on comic versions of classic stories if appropriate.

Actions for words and phrases

Asking children to create specific actions to represent words or phrases in a classic text can extend their vocabulary and develop their understanding of figurative language. It requires not only a definition of the word itself, but an understanding of what that word means in that particular context.

Creating actions for individual words and phrases can help children understand the original language and meaning of some of the older narrative poems and passages in other classic texts.

Planning and resources

- Select a short poem, fable or extract from a classic text to explore and perform.
- Using the poem or extract, underline or highlight key words or phrases in each line and divide the lines into short sections with around five to ten underlined words or phrases in each section. Then number the sections.
- All children need sight of the text with the key words underlined and the sections marked out, along with access to definitions of the underlined words.

What to do

- If necessary summarise the meaning of the poem or extract before presenting it to the children.

Model the activity

Model the following process using a combination of thinking aloud and asking the children for suggestions:

- Take the first section (number 1) and go through each underlined word or phrase in that section, asking the children to help you think of an action to represent the meaning. If you are performing a nonsense poem, some of the actions will be impressions of what the words suggest. Stress that the actions need to be simple and safe and must be performed without having to move far from the space. If the underlined word is a colour they can point to that colour in the room rather than perform an action.
- When you have agreed on the actions for this first section, read it aloud asking the children to perform the actions at the appropriate points. Read slowly to accommodate the actions.
- Repeat, reading a little faster the second time.

Group work

- Organise the children into groups of two to four.

- Allocate a section of the text to each group and ask them to create an action for each underlined word or phrase, in the way you modelled it. With large classes and/or a very short extract or poem, more than one group will be performing the same section.
- After a final practice for the groups, read the section of text aloud fairly slowly, asking groups to perform their actions at the appropriate points. Groups should remain seated during the reading and stand up when it's their turn to perform.
- Read again a little faster as children learn to anticipate when their section is coming up.

Whole class version

- Work out and perform the actions for all the sections as a whole class.

EXAMPLE 1: A POEM AT THE START OF A NOVEL

Text: *Angel's Child* **by Larraine S Harrison**

What to do

Proceed as in the overview of this section with the following adaptations:

- This short poem appears at the start of the novel *Angel's Child*. It has five short verses and is suitable for a whole class activity, where the children work with the teacher to create the mimed actions for every verse and then perform it together. Alternatively you can share the verses out amongst small groups.
- Mark it up for performance as seen in this illustration.

ANGEL'S CHILD

Section 1

In an April storm at the close of day
The Bella Rose sank off Legna Bay.
But watching not so far away
Was the Angel of the Sea.

Section 2

As a mother and baby jumped in the tide
There came a voice from the water-side.
'The sea shall never take them,' cried
The Angel of the Sea.

Figure 6.1 Book cover of *Angel's Child* by Larraine S. Harrison

Section 3

When the <u>mother</u> died upon the <u>beach</u>
The <u>Angel kissed</u> the <u>baby's cheek</u>.
'This <u>child</u> shall now be <u>mine to keep</u>'
Said the <u>Angel</u> of the <u>Sea</u>.

Section 4

The <u>child</u> was <u>happy</u> and wished to <u>stay</u>
But the Islanders <u>took the child away</u>.

'You've stolen my child and you will pay'
Cried the Angel of the Sea.

Section 5

On stormy nights, when the tide is high
You can hear the Angel's bitter cry.
'Return my child or you will die'
Cursed the Angel of the Sea.

- Ask the children to decide whether The Bella Rose in section 1 should be represented by two actions for the two words or one action for a ship. Either would be acceptable as long as it has been considered.

Reader reflections

- Ask if anyone noticed that the word Legna is Angel spelt backwards. Ask why they think the author may have chosen to do that.
- Ask: 'As readers, how do you feel about novels that start with a poem?'

Extension activities

- Watch a rehearsal of the poem Angel's Child as a song on www.youtube.com/watch?v=uVVNSPTLxecand
- Discuss differences and similarities between a poem performed as a song and a spoken version, including comparing how effective they are in communicating the meaning.

EXAMPLE 2: A SONG IN A NOVEL

Text: *James and the Giant Peach* by Roald Dahl – 'The Centipede's song'

Planning, resources and what to do

Proceed as in the overview of this section, with the following adaptations:

- Children need to be familiar with the story up to and including Chapter 14.
- Using the verses from the Centipede's song underline or highlight key words and/or phrases in each verse and provide access to definitions or access to a dictionary for the

- words the children may not know. Unusual twists on familiar words in the fifth verse may need discussing and defining as a class.
- Read the first verse and ask the whole class to suggest mimed actions for the underlined words.
- Once the actions have been decided, ask all the children to perform them as you read this first verse. Then repeat the activity with the last verse.
- Arrange the children into groups and share the remaining verses amongst the groups - one verse per group - (some groups may have the same verse as another group).
- Ask the groups to work out actions for the underlined key words in their verse.
- After a final practice, read the verses and ask groups to perform their actions when you read their verse.
- Now read all the verses a little faster, incorporating the whole class actions for the first and last verses.

> **Reader reflections**
>
> Ask: *'How do you feel about stories with songs or poems in them?'*

EXAMPLE 3: PART OF A CLASSIC POEM

Text: *The Highwayman* by Alfred Noyes

This classic poem presents an opportunity to use actions to extend children's vocabulary and explore figurative language, especially metaphors like the references to the road as a ribbon found in different parts of the poem and repeated again at the end.

Proceed as in the overview of this section, with the following adaptations:

Planning and resources

What to do

- Explain to the children that they will be asked to perform parts of the poem using mimed actions to express some of the words and phrases.
- Use the opening three lines to model the process with the whole class, paying particular attention to the metaphors and their contexts.

Group work

- Use a different extract from the poem for the group work, such as where Tim overhears the Highwayman talking to Bess and focus on this section for the reading and performance.
- Proceed as in the overview.

> **Reader reflections**
>
> Use the 'where do you stand now?' spider's web strategy to open up discussion on the statement *'actions help an audience understand a poem.'* Children stand in a circle around the person making the statement. They then move closer to them according to how far they agree with the statement.

Extension activities

- Explore how to read other short sections of this poem in different ways, such as using sound effects for the marching troops, the wind, the sound of horses' hooves on the cobbles, the whip and the whistled tune or direct speech for the Highwayman talking to Bess.

EXAMPLE 4: *RIDING A LION* FROM THE COLLECTION OF POEMS *RIDING A LION* BY CORAL RUMBLE

What to do

Proceed as in the overview of this section, with the following adaptations:

- Use the first three lines of this short poem to model the process.
- Underline pairs of words as well as individual ones, to bring out the meaning e.g. *tented ribs* and *clinging knees*.
- This poem is full of interesting vocabulary, so groups may only need one line each to have enough underlined words. Alternatively the actions for the whole poem could be performed by all the class.

Extension activity

Choose another short poem from this collection such as **On Why You Shouldn't Catch a Witch's Cackle** or **Disappointed Frog** and ask groups of children to underline their own words for their actions. Then read the chosen poems aloud as they all perform their different actions.

Further Suggestions

Crocodile Tears by Roger McGough: Children create actions for the quirky invented words in this book and use as a model to make up words to incorporate into their own poems.

Choral reading with actions

When choral reading (i.e. children reading aloud in unison) is performed with actions, children have to engage with the meaning of the text to know exactly when and how to join in. Actions for some of the words in a nonsense poem will reflect the context but are open to individual interpretations. In this case children will perform different actions according to their individual responses.

Short extracts from poems or fables can be learnt by heart and read chorally by all the class, along with the actions. Parts of longer poems or fables can be read by the teacher with children providing choral readings with actions at given points. Encourage children to enjoy and savour the different types of sounds in the actual words such the effects of assonance, alliteration and onomatopoeia.

EXAMPLE 1: *THE JUMBLIES* BY EDWARD LEAR ILLUSTRATED BY IAN BECK

Planning and resources

- Children will need sight of the poem during the activity, so they can read the text as they perform.

What to do

- Invite the children to help you perform a reading of the poem with actions, sound effects and choral reading.
- Practise chorally reading the repeated refrain: *Far and few, far and few . . . etc.*
- Start the reading with a group performing a freeze-frame of the moment the Jumblies left, watched by their sceptical friends, referred to in the poem as *Everyone*. Finish with another freeze-frame of the moment *Everyone* drank their health when the Jumblies returned. Ask the children in the freeze-frames to speak out their character's thoughts (see Chapter 5).
- Go through each verse and work with the children to identify opportunities for actions and sound effects.
- Allocate two different groups to read the direct speech spoken by the Jumblies and *Everyone*. Those speaking as the Jumblies could stand together in a group as if in the sieve.
- Practise putting it all together and then perform without stopping.
- Record the reading and/or perform it live for other children.

EXAMPLE 2: *SLUDGE-BOG STEW* BY SUE HARDY DAWSON FROM *WHERE ZEBRAS GO*

This poem has some interesting vocabulary like *doppelganger* and *super-slammer* that can be explored and performed with actions, as well as a repeated chorus for choral reading.

Proceed in a similar way to Example 1 using the repeated chorus in this poem, which changes slightly at the end.

EXAMPLE 3: *AESOP'S FABLES* ILLUSTRATED BY HARRISON WEIR ET AL.

- Recite parts of fables chorally with actions, pausing for individual children to recite the direct speech e.g. Town Mouse and Country Mouse or read a shorter fable chorally e.g. Crying Wolf Too Often.
- Perform fables alongside modern versions such as the poem **Between The Wolf And The Dog** by James Carter (from **Weird, Wild and Wonderful**) based on Aesop's fable *The Dog and the Wolf*.

Performing poems on a similar theme

Performing poems on a similar theme demonstrates how similar ideas can be expressed in different ways.

Planning, resources and what to do

- Make a list of performance possibilities with the class and let the children contribute to the planning, either as a whole class and/or in smaller groups as appropriate. They can use actions, choral reading, groups reading parts and making sound effects, individuals reading direct speech and any other ideas they might want to add to the list.
- The whole class can perform all the poems or different poems can be allocated to different groups, depending on the length of the poems and the confidence of the children. Most children benefit from working on at least one poem with the whole class as a model. Some poetry collections such as **Poems to Perform** by Julia Donaldson include ideas for performance that children could consider in their planning.

EXAMPLE 1: FOOTBALL POEMS

Texts:
- *What Can You Do with a Football?* by James Carter from *Weird, Wild and Wonderful*
- *The School Goalie's Reasons* and *The Third Team* by Brian Moses from *The Great Galactic*
- *Mute* by Sue Hardy Dawson from *Where Zebras Go*
- *Unfair* by Michael Rosen and *The Man Who Invented Football* by Kit Wright from *The Puffin Book of Utterly Brilliant Poetry* edited by Brian Patten
- *Football Mad* by Benjamin Zephaniah in *Poems to Perform* by Julia Donaldson

What to do

- Work out and perform these poems in different ways as a whole class or model some first then allocate others to groups.
- Compare the poems according to different criteria e.g. how the words reflect their meanings, how easy they are to understand, how appealing they are to football followers and those who know nothing about the game etc.

Extension activity

- Either as a class or as individuals, children create a poem based on a different sport or activity. They should use the poems they performed as a stimulus or a model.

EXAMPLE 2: CONTRASTING CREATURES

Texts: *A Sloth's Diary* and *Dave* by Coral Rumble from *Riding A Lion*

What to do

- Perform these two poems about a sloth and a dolphin in different ways. Look at the way the poems are written differently to reflect the way the creatures move.
- The different diary days for the Sloth can be read very slowly by different groups, followed by all the class chorally reading the phrase *Sleep Do it Tomorrow* each time.
- Then ask groups to read different verses of Dave at a fairly rapid pace to reflect the movements, using actions for some of the words that reflect these movements e.g. *zigging and zagging*.

Further Suggestions

Caring for the planet:

Use different ways to perform these poems about caring for the planet and then compare them:

- ***The Beautiful Planet*** and ***Planet for Sale*** by Sue Hardy-Dawson from ***Where Zebras Go***
- ***Sweet Meadow, Who Cares*** and ***Tree*** by James Carter from ***Weird, Wild*** and ***Wonderful***

Performing riddles

Creating mimed actions to illustrate and perform riddles means children have to slow down the delivery to focus on the meanings of the words. It also encourages children to

Ages 7-11 (Years 2-6)

enjoy, savour and play with language to foster a fascination for word play and the meanings of words.

Planning and resources

- Select texts representing a selection of riddles such as:

The Silly Book of Weird and Wacky Words by Andy Seed
I Am a Jigsaw by Roger Stevens
Poetry Alive. Footprints in the Butter edited by Pie Corbett
Spot the Fairy Tales (Ten Tiny Senru) by James Carter from *Weird, Wild and Wonderful*

- Children need access to dictionaries or access to definitions of unfamiliar words.

You will need:

- Enough examples of riddles for pairs of children. If you are asking a guided reading group to select the examples you will need multiple copies of one text or enough copies of different texts for the group.

What to do

Version 1: Guided Reading

- Children in the guided reading group are given the task of browsing the texts to identify and select riddles suitable for the class to perform with actions at a later time.
- Discuss the characteristics of riddles and how to identify them.
- After discussing a few examples and identifying any unfamiliar vocabulary, ask the children to browse the text(s) to select riddles where the words or phrases could be acted out in mime during the reading.
- Use these examples as extracts for the whole class to perform as in Version 2.

Version 2: whole class work

- Explain that the challenge is for pairs to create and mime actions whilst reading or saying the riddle aloud. Children choose whether one will read/ tell the riddle, whilst the other mimes the actions or they both read chorally and mime at the same time.
- Talk about the characteristics of a riddle with reference to the texts.
- After sharing a few examples, hand out copies of riddles for pairs to work out the actions for the highlighted words or phrases. Encourage children to look up the meanings of any words they are not sure of in order to create the appropriate actions. More confident children may benefit from the opportunity to highlight their own words or phrases.
- Allow time to practise before inviting pairs to perform their riddles by reading or saying the words and performing the actions in whatever way they have chosen.
- Allow time for the class to guess the answers to the riddles.

Reader reflections

Ask: *'Did the actions add or detract from the meaning and enjoyment of the riddle for the audience when read or spoken aloud? Why do you think this?'*

Extension activities

Link to the riddles in Chapter 5 of **The Hobbit by J. R. R. Tolkien** ('Riddles in the dark'). Talk about the history of riddles and links to folk songs. Use this as an opportunity to discuss how riddles in the past sometimes had hidden meanings linked to serious issues.

Point out how riddles often use imagery and metaphors for effect.

Invite children to use the texts as models for writing their own riddles, perhaps based on familiar objects such as those in school.

Improvisations

Inviting a group to improvise a scene from a story in front of the class can provide an engaging focus for discussion about deeper meanings within the text. However, whilst those children who enjoy performing should be given opportunities to do so, some find it a stressful experience. Short spontaneous improvisations as part of a lesson, shared as overheard snippets or presented as a freeze-frame coming to life for a few seconds are often less daunting. Whole class improvisations led by a teacher-in-role also provide a way to include all the children.

Time to think and plan prior to improvising, with an element of choice as to what and how much they are expected to say, usually helps cautious children feel more comfortable about the prospect. Time to polish or script improvisations before performing them can also help.

Clear expectations that no one child should dominate in a group improvisation encourages children to work together to produce the drama.

Planning, resources and what to do

- Choose an extract from a story or event where there is a dilemma or a moment of tension e.g. moments where children can improvise what might happen next, what happened before, what happened off camera or what might happen if. . . ?
- Children need to be familiar with the chosen extract either before or after the activity, depending on the context.
- If appropriate, plan a suitable line to start the improvisation e.g.

  I've got something to tell/ ask you . . .
  What are you thinking about right now? What do you think about . . . ?

What shall we do about . . . ?
How are you feeling?
Why did you/they do that?
I need some advice . . .

- The ability to co-operate with others needs to be a consideration when assigning children to groups for improvised drama, but offering some form of guidance can also help. The amount and nature of the guidance will depend on the needs of the children, but could include some or all of the following.

    1   Improvisations should be in line with school values.
    2   Physical contact should be avoided due to lack of time to rehearse safely.
    3   Everyone should be given a chance to say something and no-one should dominate.
    4   Show respect and keep everyone safe.

- If children are working in groups, give a time limit for the preparation and the length of the final improvisation.
- Decide if and how group improvisations will be shared with the rest of the class. You can ask groups to select, polish and recreate snippets to perform or ask them to choose a significant moment to present as a freeze-frame with thoughts. Alternatively they can just report back on what happened.
- If only one group is performing in front of the class, freeze the improvisation occasionally to allow the children watching to respond or make suggestions on how the scene might develop.

EXAMPLE: *THE VALLEY OF LOST SECRETS* BY LESLEY PARR

What to do

- This activity is designed as an introduction to the book.
- Read out the first sentence on the back cover: *'When is Jimmy evacuated to a small village in Wales, it couldn't be more different from London.'*
- Talk briefly about evacuees in the context of the Second World War and then discuss how the statement on the back cover could be both positive and negative e.g. *'How was the Welsh village different from London? What might the evacuees be looking forward to and what might they be concerned about?'*
- Arrange the children in pairs or small groups to improvise a conversation between the evacuees as they travelled to Wales on the train.
- After sharing some ideas, give children a few minutes in silence to decide what they might be feeling and thinking on the train.
- Allocate one child in each group to start the conversation but stress that everyone should have a chance to make a contribution to the improvisation to bring out the evacuees' feelings.
- The improvisation should last a few minutes and should stop when you say *'freeze.'*
- After the improvisation ask groups to report back on what the evacuees were feeling, before starting to read the text.

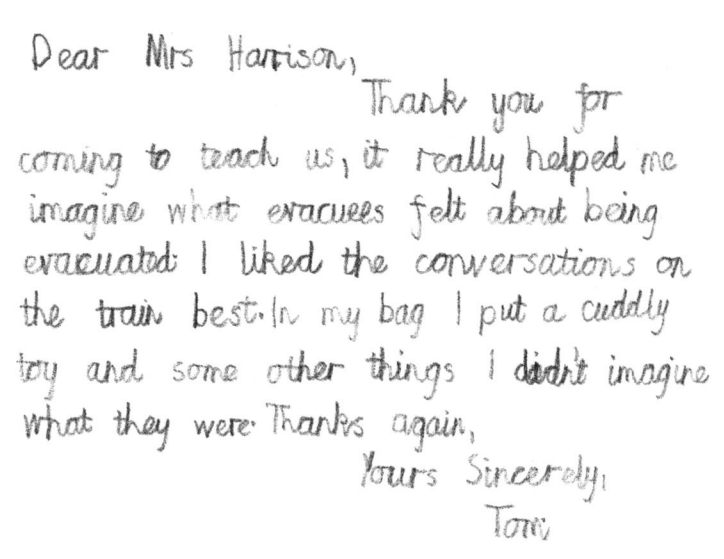

> Dear Mrs Harrison,
> Thank you for coming to teach us, it really helped me imagine what evacuees felt about being evacuated. I liked the conversations on the train best. In my bag I put a cuddly toy and some other things I didn't imagine what they were. Thanks again,
> Yours Sincerely,
> Tom

Figure 6.2 A child's letter about evacuees

On air

Participating in a real or imaginary live radio broadcast for a recording is an exciting and motivating prospect for most children. It avoids the need for a visual performance, but puts more emphasis on vocal skills, either improvised or reading from a script. A radio broadcast provides audience and purpose for reading playscripts which demands reading with expression with attention to the meaning. If the broadcast hosts a drama where children play characters linked to a story or information books, the need to read in preparation also creates audience and purpose for reading for meaning. This can occur whether the radio show is real or imagined.

Some schools have their own radio stations which have a positive impact on literacy and other areas of learning across the whole school. Progress in technology means this is now more of an option than it used to be and well worth investigating. (See the appendix for more information about setting up and using a radio station in school.)

A real live school radio station offers the best experience for drama, but it's possible to stage a near-authentic radio broadcasting experience with just a laptop or recording device. Recording an imaginary radio show for the class to listen to later is more effective if it's made to appear as authentic as possible. Sharing insider knowledge and tips from radio broadcasters will help make an imaginary radio show feel even more real. These include such things as stock sentences on the wall, off-script banter and the need for smooth handovers etc.

The choice of radio show you create will depend on the type of text you wish to focus on. Information texts can be fed into a radio show called *Fascinating Facts* featuring the children as experts, whereas children in role as eye-witnesses to events in stories can be interviewed during a fictitious news report. Children can also adapt snippets of scripted plays for radio performances.

Planning and resources

- Arrange the children into groups of about three or four. At least one child in each group needs to be comfortable with reading or talking aloud for a recording.
- If you are using information texts, each group will need access to the texts to prepare for the show.
- If you are using a story then children will need sight of the relevant parts of the story in preparation for the show. If you are interviewing eye-witnesses for the news, you will need to prepare the questions they will be asked.
- If the children are reading from all or part of a scripted play, they will need time beforehand to discuss how to adapt it for radio and time to rehearse.
- You will need a space to represent the recording studio with a device to record the show, a table with a sign saying 'mic live' and another saying 'on air' (you can purchase illuminated 'on air' signs fairly cheaply to add authenticity). You will also need chairs for the presenters and a timer. Other props are optional.

What to do

Preparation: reading and rehearsal

- Arrange the children in their groups.
- Explain that you are going to record a show in the performance space, as if it were a live radio broadcast. Share the name and purpose of the show and invite the children to take part in their groups. Each group will present for a short time, with an introduction and conclusion from yourself as the host.
- Emphasise that when the 'mic live' sign is put up, it will be like a real live radio broadcast with a requirement for silence and no undo button. Dialogue may be scripted or unscripted and can include *off script banter* but if things go wrong they must be resilient, cover it and carry on. Talk about how radio presenters often have useful phrases on the wall of their studios to help them, especially if things don't go as expected e.g. 'Still to come on the show,' 'So that's it from me. Next up is,' 'Hope you are enjoying the show so far . . . we will be with you again soon.' Invite the children to think of some more phrases and write them up so everyone can see and use them if necessary.
- Most children are keen to be on air but if any are very unwilling or unable to take part they can help prepare the research and support any rehearsals.
- The decision as to whether the children should script their words or make notes to help them improvise depends on the context and the needs of the class. They may also prefer to use tablets or iPads rather than written paper scripts (See appendix).
- If you are using information texts, ask groups to read through their texts to find some interesting facts or items they can present within the given time slot.
- If you are basing the show on interviewing eye witnesses to an event in a story, you will need to share the questions the host will be asking, so groups can prepare their responses.
- The exact time slot for each group depends on the confidence of the children, the size of the class and how long you want the playback to last, but working to a time slot is a good discipline that adds authenticity and encourages conciseness.

'Timing is essential, you can't replicate a performance if you don't know how long it should take. On average ninety words should take about sixty seconds to read' (Russell Prue: Radio Broadcaster).

- Allow plenty of time for research and practising the presentations within the time limits.
- Agree the order of presentations.

The radio show

- Put a child in charge of the 'mic live' sign. When it's displayed everyone else should be silent.
- Put a child in charge of the timer, giving a non-verbal signal when the time is up.
- Either pause the recording between groups to allow the next group to come to the studio or play it like a live broadcast where the children need to be ready to change over.
- Children usually enjoy the pressure of producing a live recording, whether for a real show or an imagined one and enjoy hearing it played back. Try to avoid a situation where children criticise each other's performances. Instead invite children to assess to what extent the show provided useful and/or interesting information about the texts.

EXAMPLE 1: RADIO SHOWS BASED ON INFORMATION TEXTS

Text: *WHAT A WASTE* by Jess French.

Planning, resources and what to do

- Proceed as previously described, with a show called *Fascinating Facts about Waste*. In this show the children present their facts in role as experts and/or researchers.
- Make copies of separate pages from the text **What A Waste.** This book has several pages on different aspects of Waste, each with clearly identifiable facts. Groups choose a few facts from their given page or pages. They should start by announcing the title of their page each time.
- Some of the presentations will be shorter as there are fewer facts on some pages, so allocate the texts to suit the children.
- Encourage children to present their facts clearly but in interesting ways to keeping the interest of the listeners.

Extension activity

- Children put together a real or imaginary radio show for younger children on the same topic, simplifying the facts and finishing with one group sharing the reading of a short story on the same topic e.g. ***Dinosaurs and All That Rubbish* by Michael Foreman.**

EXAMPLE 2: RADIO SHOWS BASED ON STORIES

Proceed as in the overview of ON AIR with shows that can be linked to stories such the following:

- *The Rascally Cake* by Jeanne Willis and Korky Paul

    Record a show called '**How to Make a Rascally Cake.**'

After sharing ideas in pairs, work as a class to write a menu of disgusting ingredients, similar to those in the rascally cake. Either read it yourself as the show host, or share the reading with the children.

- *Oliver and the Seawigs* by Philip Reeve

Record a show called '**How to Create a Seawig.**' After sharing ideas in pairs, work with the class to produce a script that you and/or a few children can read out on the show.

- *Malamander* by Thomas Taylor

Record a **travel show** where children in role as live broadcasters interview others in role as residents of Eerie-on-Sea about the bookshop, the hotel and the legend of the Malamander.

Performing and presenting playscripts

Playscripts are texts written with performance in mind. If children are to appreciate the full meaning of the play and what makes a playscript different from a story, they need to become involved in that performance in some way. Performing and presenting a play may involve directing, supporting or acting, but each role brings with it the need to read the play for meaning with a clear sense of audience and purpose.

Taking part in a whole school production provides children with a valuable and often memorable experience, but one which, due to the amount of time and work involved, is often limited to a couple of times a year.

Short plays or extracts however mean that teachers have more time to focus on the quality and features of a playscript, rather than having to manage a full production. Focusing on a short scene means children become more familiar with the language and meaning of the script through rehearsals. It also allows more time to read or learn lines, create props and costumes for a visual performance or create sound effects for a radio performance.

If the play is an adaptation of a novel, a short scene can be compared to the same event in the novel. Some short playscripts are versions of classic plays and stories, presenting melodramatic fun versions sprinkled with original lines to engage and inspire children to want to learn more. Others focus on characters in reading schemes or link to other areas of the curriculum, such as history.

The experience of a playscript needs to include some consideration of the stage set, costumes and/or sound effects, along with the stage directions. It should also involve some appreciation of how to perform in terms of voice and expression. Radio versions of plays also

Actions and performances 119

need adapting to the lack of visual clues. All this is more achievable with a short play or scene and will provide a good model for children writing their own playscripts.

Planning and resources

- Select a short playscript or a short scene from a longer play, so all children have an opportunity to either play a part or contribute to the performance in another way.
- All children need copies of or sight of the play or scene.
- A cleared area for the performance.
- Resources to make versions of props or costumes specifically mentioned in the play and/or any sound effects if appropriate.
- A device to record the final performance if appropriate.

What to do

Introducing the plot and the themes

- The best way to introduce a playscript is to engage the children with the story, especially if the plot is complicated. Some plays, particularly those with simple plots for younger children or versions of familiar novels, need little introduction. Melodramatic versions of classic plays and stories also need little introduction as they involve simple versions of the original plots.

However if the script needs more explanation, children can be given snippets to discover some of the plot themselves, watch a film version or be given a summary. The Silent Movie drama strategy can also provide a useful overview of a complicated plot.

The roles

- Discuss the wide range of equally important roles needed for performing and presenting a play in a theatre, including set designers, costume and prop makers, sound engineers, lighting engineers and directors as well as the actors. Simplify this for younger children, but emphasise how a play in a theatre or on radio requires a team effort to achieve a good performance.
- Talk about the importance of the audience and how directors and those working on the set and production have to adapt to suit both the performance space and the audience.
- Talk about how to adapt this performance for a school audience in the classroom, with the resources available.
- Allocate the acting and non-acting parts, making sure children are comfortable with their roles and able to manage any reading.
- Auditions for acting parts are not essential for a short class play where the teacher knows the children and time is short.
- Ask the actors to highlight their lines on their scripts and ask others to highlight any stage directions or set changes etc.

The first reading

- Conduct the first reading sitting down. Run straight through with as few pauses as possible to get a sense of the whole. When working with younger children it may be best to read most of the script to the children yourself first.

Exploring the characters

- Some of the drama strategies in Chapter 7 such as role-on-the-wall and the character circle, can help children look deeper into each character's personality, appearance, thoughts, feelings, relationships and motivations during the play. This should include the minor and non-speaking parts. Including the minor characters provides an opportunity to speculate on their purpose and the writer's intent.
- Make a freeze-frame of the first moment of the performance, using forum theatre to help make decisions about where the actors would stand based on what they know of the play. Then ask what each character might be thinking and feeling at that moment (see Chapter 5).

Reading with clarity and expression

- **The Echo**: Stand at the front of the class with the script and read out a few of the lines one at a time, asking the class to echo them. Make deliberate mistakes for the children to identify e.g. read facing away from the audience, with head down, too quietly, shouting to distort the words, too fast, very slow, without expression.
- Emphasise the need to read with meaning and appropriate expression. If the play is a fun melodramatic version there is scope for improvisation, but the lines and the way they are spoken should reflect the meaning of the original script. The words need to be heard clearly in whatever form, so advise children to speak clearly and slightly slower than if they were saying the words in real life and project their voice as if they were speaking to someone at the back of the room. Talk about the need to *share* the lines with the audience rather than just reading them out.
- Give the actors time to practise their lines in small groups, whilst the others work in groups on set, costume, sound, props etc

(Optional) The dress rehearsal

- Rehearse the play as if it were a final performance and make any last-minute changes.

The final performance

Options for performing the play:

a   Allow actors time to memorise their lines and perform the play at a later date.
b   Perform a walk-through version with actors reading from scripts.
c   Prepare and record an audio version with sound effects and actors reading from scripts.

Reflection

- To protect children's self-esteem, ask each child to consider their *own* performance or contribution, including non-acting roles. Each child should identify one aspect of their work they thought went well and one aspect they might improve if they had more time. Whether this is written and/or shared with the class will depend on the needs of the children.

> **Reader reflections**
>
> Invite the children to pick out the main differences between a play and a novel, along with reasons why they have these different features.

EXAMPLE 1: A PLAY BASED ON A NOVEL

Texts:

- *Roald Dahl's Charlie and the Chocolate Factory: A Play* adapted by Richard George
- *Charlie and the Chocolate Factory* by Roald Dahl

Planning and resources

- Children need to be familiar with the novel up to and including Chapter 25 ('The Great Glass Lift').
- Children need sight of Chapter 25 of the novel after the performance.

You will need:

- Copies of the playscript, up to and including Scene 9 ('In the Great Glass Elevator') – one for each child.
- A cleared performance area.
- Items for simple costumes and props such as scarves, caps, waistcoats, ties, a walking stick, a few craft materials.
- Adhesive name labels for the characters in Scene 9.

What to do

Proceed as in the overview, with the following adaptations:

- Allocate the acting parts, making sure the children are comfortable with their assigned roles and can manage the reading.

- Read through the play up to and including Scene 9, making sure children understand the story up to that point.
- Talk about how the actors might move at certain points to reflect the elevator experience.

Comparisons with the novel

- Look at Chapter 25 in the novel and ask the children to identify any differences between the events in this chapter and the play version. Discuss why changes may have been made to the scripted version.

Further suggestions for plays adapted from novels by Roald Daahl:

Read all or parts of the following plays by Roald Dahl and select a scene to perform. Then compare that scene with the equivalent events in the novel:

- *The BFG: A Play* by David Wood
- *Danny Champion of the World: A Play* by David Wood
- *Fantastic Mr. Fox: A Play* by Sally Reid
- *James and the Giant Peach: A Play* by Richard George
- *The Twits: A Play* by David Wood
- *The Witches: A Play* by David Wood

EXAMPLE 2: HISTORICAL PLAYS

Text: *Sausages for Tea* by Alison Chaplin

Set in November 1940, this short playscript is about evacuees at home after the *'Phoney War'* in England during the Second World War. It includes advice on props, costume and staging, an introduction to the historical context and some follow up activities.

Planning, resources and what to do

- Proceed as in Example 1 but replace the novel with information texts about the *'Phoney War'* and rationing. Make comparisons between the way this information is communicated in books and in a play and consider which, if any, is more effective and why.

Further suggestions for historical plays:

- *Bombs and Blackberries* by Julia Donaldson
- *Putting on a Play: Gunpowder Plot* by Tony Bradman
- *Viking Adventures* by Roderick Hunt

EXAMPLE 3: FUN WITH SHAKESPEARE AND OTHER CLASSICS

Text: *Playing with Plays* **by Brendan P. Kelso**

These are short melodramatic versions of classic plays and stories for three different group sizes within each book. Titles include Shakespeare's most popular plays like *Macbeth*, *Hamlet* and *A Midsummer Night's Dream* and classic stories such as *Treasure Island* and *Oliver Twist*. With highlighted sections containing a sprinkling of the original text, they provide an insight into the meaning of classic plays and stories in a fun and engaging way.

Further suggestions for playscripts

- *25 Science Plays for Beginning Readers* **by Sheryl Ann Crawford** (more suited to Years 2/3)
- *Let's Perform* **by Cath Howe**
- *Playtime* **by Julia Donaldson**

7 Exploring characters

LINKS TO READING FOR MEANING: characters' thoughts, feelings, problems, motives and intentions; relationships between characters; comparing characters within and across books; authorial intent and viewpoint; fact and opinion; predictions; different perspectives; empathy; inference; appropriate questioning; engaging with fiction and information texts; conversations about books; forming and justifying opinions about texts.

Rationale

This chapter suggests how variations on some of the most well-known drama strategies can help children to explore the motivations, relationships, feelings and thoughts of characters, both real and imagined including links to information texts. All the activities are designed to take place in a classroom to complement ongoing work on reading for meaning, but can also form part of a longer whole group drama lesson.

Contents

Role-on-the-wall	125
Variations on hot-seating	132
The character circle	137
Spotlighting/overheard conversations	141
The line-up	144

Drama strategies

Character circle
Hot-seating
Improvisation
Line-up
Role-on-the wall
Spotlighting/Overheard conversations
Teacher-in-role

DOI: 10.4324/9781003250777-10

Exploring characters

Role-on-the-wall

Whilst role-on-the-wall traditionally applies to fictional characters in a text, it can also be applied to non-fiction texts where the character is or was a real person such as a historical figure or an author. It can also be applied to animals and other creatures described in information texts. Even some abstract scientific or geographical concepts can be personified as a role-on-the-wall if appropriate.

Planning and resources

- Select a character from a text and a point in time for the exploration of that character. The children need to be familiar with the text up to that point.
- Children need access to extracts of the text that portray the character.

You will need:

- An outline of the character drawn on a large sheet of paper or a screen. If there is an image of the character in the text, you can project it onto paper and trace round it. Various templates are also available from online resources. Groups of characters or abstract concepts can be represented by using a simple shape.
- (Optional) Individual whiteboards.
- (Optional) A scarf or similar simple item of clothing as a sign of teacher-in-role.

What to do

- Display the role-on-the wall outline and write the character's name on it.

The basic strategy

- Working in pairs, ask the children to find words e.g. adjectives, noun phrases or a phrase from the text, which reveal something about the character. Alternatively they can think of their own words to describe the character based on their reading of the text. They should write these down on individual whiteboards or paper. Ask one of each pair to share the words on their whiteboards or feedback verbally. Encourage them to refer to the text to justify their choices. This can be direct evidence or inferential evidence. Summarise the responses then discuss and agree what words you should write inside the outline to describe the character.

Other versions:

1. **Facts and opinions:** Write what the children know about the character inside the outline (facts) and what they think of the character round the outside (opinions).
2. **What characters say:** Record what a character says or thinks about themselves inside the outline and what other characters say or think about them round the outside.
3. **Thoughts and feelings:** Consider what the character might be thinking at a specific point in the text. Record their thoughts inside the head section of the outline. Then

consider what they might be feeling and record these inside the body section or within a heart shape inside the body. Icons expressing different emotions can also be added if appropriate.

4   **Physical description and personality:** Draw a line down the centre of the outline. Write phrases from the text describing what the character looks like on one side of the outline and those describing their personality on the other.

5   **Broader perspectives:** In the same way as version 4, draw a line down the centre of the outline to record the character's friends and enemies, secrets and dreams or likes and dislikes etc.

6   **Exploration:** Write questions for *'What we want to know about the character'* around the outside of the outline and fill in the answers as you read more of the text.

7   **Predictions:** Write *'What we predict/expect to happen to this character'* inside the outline and tick off any that turn out to be correct.

8   **Vocabulary:** Provide a choice of pre-written words or a word bank of character descriptions to write in the outline and blank ones for children to add their own.

9   **Symbols:** Children suggest and record relevant symbols or images for the character inside the outline. Ask *'Why have you chosen these?'* and link to the text.

10 **Relationships:** Complete roles-on-the-wall for two characters from the same story who have some kind of relationship. Join the outlines with arrows. Write words along the arrows to reveal their relationship and/or what they think of each other.

11 **Comparing characters:** Complete and compare roles-on-the-wall for key characters from different stories. Write words inside the outlines to describe their similarities and words outside the outlines to describe their differences. It may be useful to think about particular criteria e.g. physical appearance, personality, environment, family circumstances etc. For example, compare and contrast the family circumstances of April in **The Last Bear by Hannah Gold,** Blue Wing in **The Shark Caller by Zillah Bethell** and Megan in **Red Snow by Larraine S Harrison.**

12 **Character development:** Use role-on-the-wall early in the reading, then leave on display to track character development as the children read more of the story e.g. how characters like Plop in **The Owl Who Was Afraid of the Dark by Jill Tomlinson** and Hector in **The Night Bus Hero by Onjali Q. Rauf** change as their story progresses.

13 **Groups of characters:** Draw a circle to represent a defined group with a key role to play in a story, such as the mechanicals in **Cogheart by Peter Bunzl.** Record the common features of that group inside the circle and then discuss if any members of the group differ from the others in key ways.

14 **Setting-on-the-wall:** Draw a representative outline of the setting such as a simple house or tree outline and write descriptive words about the setting from the text inside the outlines.

15 **Book-on-the-wall:** Draw an outline of a class book that children are about to read. Write inside what the children know from the cover and blurb. Then write questions on what they want to know or are not sure about and/or predictions around the outside. Tick off the questions and/or add more details as you read and discover more.

16. **Author-on-the-wall:** Children collect and record facts about an author inside a basic head and shoulders outline and write what they think about their books around the outside.
17. **Favourites-on-the wall:** Children draw and complete basic outlines of their favourite characters, with reasons why they like them written inside.
18. **Creatures-on-the wall:** Children draw an outline of a creature or an outline of its habitat. They research and then record information such as what it eats and any other interesting facts inside the outline and what they think of the creature outside the outline. This could also apply to a group of creatures with common features such as those with claws.
19. **Guess who?** Children work in pairs to produce small role-on-the-wall outlines of a character of their choice from a well-known story. They use adjectives to describe the character's appearance on one side and their personality on the other but do not mention the character's name. The teacher collects and displays the outlines and/or they are read out for the class to guess who the characters are.

Reader reflections

Ask:

- 'What do you, as the readers, feel about the character(s) on the wall?'
- 'Who is your favourite character in this story and why?'
- 'Did your feelings or opinions of any of the characters change as you read the story?'
- 'What other stories have you read where characters change or develop during the story?'

Extension activities

- Allow the class to vote on which character they would like to explore next via role-on-the-wall.
- Children create their own role-on-the-page version of another character or a favourite character from a book they have read themselves.
- Use the role-on-the-wall words and phrases as a basis for creative activities such as dance, music, songs, poetry, stories or art work to represent the character.
- Use teacher-in-role as someone who knows the character depicted on the role-on-the-wall, such as a neighbour, parent or friend. In this role, talk about your opinions of the character and ask the children if they feel the same.

Adaptations for distance learning

- Collect and record children's verbal responses about a character on a role-on-the-screen.
- Record a demonstration of role-on-the-wall, so children can create their own role-on-the-page versions for a different character from the text and share them during distance learning.

EXAMPLE 1: *GEORGE'S MARVELLOUS MEDICINE* BY ROALD DAHL

Planning and resources

- Children need to be familiar with the first Chapter entitled 'Grandma' and have access to this part of the text before reading the rest of the book.

You will need:

- A role-on-the-wall outline to represent Grandma, drawn on a large sheet of paper or on a screen.
- (Optional) A range of words on display, describing personalities, feelings, physical characteristics etc
- (Optional) A scarf or other small item of clothing to represent George in one of the extension activities.

What to do

- Read the story to the end of Chapter 1 entitled 'Grandma.'
- Display the role-on-the-wall outline of Grandma and select one of the following versions:
    1. Write what readers know about Grandma up to this point in the story inside the outline and then add what the children think of her and her behaviour around the outside.
    2. Draw a line down the middle of the outline. Write what Grandma looks like on one side and what sort of person she is on the other side.
    3. Use symbols or thumbnail sketches to describe Grandma's behaviour and display around the outline.

> ### Reader reflections
>
> Use the strategy '**where do you stand now?**' by placing 'agree' and 'disagree' cards on opposite sides of the room to ask the children: *'Does this first chapter about Grandma make you want to read the rest of the book?'*
>
> Those who are uncertain should stand in the middle of the room. Then ask some of the children to explain the reason for their choice.

Extension activities

- **Teacher-in-role:** Ask the children to pretend you are George when you wear the scarf. On the word '*action*' take on the role as George and explain how you feel about Grandma. Tell the children about your plan to make a new medicine to make her less grumpy. Ask them what might go in the medicine to calm Grandma down. Use the word '*freeze*' as you take off the scarf to end the activity. Make a list of the children's ideas for the ingredients of the medicine. Read the next chapter entitled 'The Marvellous Plan' to find out what ingredients George actually used.
- Take a vote to decide on another character from the book to explore via role-on-the-wall.
- Complete a role-on-the-wall for George, or ask children to do their own role-on-the-page version.
- Make a role-on-the-wall for Granny Regurgita based on the description at the start of **The Nothing to See Here Hotel** by **Steven Butler** and compare with George's Grandma.

Adaptations for distance learning

After reading the first chapter to the children, complete a screen version of role-on-the-wall as previously described.

EXAMPLE 2: *VARJAK PAW* BY S. F. SAID

Planning and resources

- Children will need to be familiar with the story up to the end of Chapter 7, followed by the rest of the story after the activity.

You will need:

- A large outline of Varjak or a simple outline of a cat drawn on a sheet of paper or on a screen.
- A large piece of dark coloured plain material or a blanket to cover a chair.

What to do

- Read the text up to the end of Chapter 7.
- Display the role-on-the-wall outline and label it as a representation of Varjak.
- Working in pairs, ask children to write down a few words or phrases to describe Varjak up to this point in the text. These can be their own words and/or words from the text.

- Draw a line down the centre with the labels 'physical description' and 'personality' on either side of the line, then add the words 'what we think' around the outside. Work with the children to write words or phrases in the appropriate places on the role-on-the-wall. Use this as a basis for discussion on the character of Varjak up to this point.
- Set up teacher-in-role as Jalal's voice: Place the blanket on a chair and ask the children to imagine that you are the voice of Jalal when sitting in this chair. Use the words *'action'* and *'freeze'* to start and stop this activity.
- It's not advisable to change your voice as this could be a distraction, but you may want to talk in a more formal tone, consistent with the character. In Jalal's voice, explain your view of Varjak at the end of Chapter 7, and why you behaved in the way you did when you met him. Talk about your hopes and fears for Varjak in the future. Then ask the children their opinion, based on what they know of Varjak.
- Come out of role to discuss this further. Talk about how characters can change during the course of a novel. Introduce the idea that the words on the role-on-the-wall may need to be adapted as the story progresses. If appropriate, talk about and record any predictions alongside the outline.
- Leave the role-on-the-wall on display as you read the rest of the story. Stop at various points, to ask the children if they would like to adapt any of the words/comments or tick off any predictions as they see Varjak's character developing. Check evidence from the text before adapting anything.
- **Setting-on-the wall**: Draw an outline of a cityscape and a simple outline of a house to represent the two different settings in the story and write descriptive words about the settings inside them. Then make comparisons and link to the impact of the change of setting on Varjak's character and story events.

> **Reader reflections**
>
> Ask:
>
> - 'As readers, do you find it hard to accept that the main character is a cat who talks to other cats? If not, why not?'
> - 'What other children's novels do you know that are based on animal characters who narrate the story?'
>
> Compare **Varjak Paw** to other books written from an animal's perspective such as the dog in **I Cosmo** or the cat in **My Life as a Cat by Carlie Sorosiak** and the fox in **Fantastic Mr. Fox by Roald Dahl**.
>
> Ask: 'How are these different from stories **about** an animal, such as **The Last Bear by Hannah Gold** or **Born to Run by Michael Morpurgo**?'

Exploring characters

Extension activities

- Children produce their own role-on-the-page versions for another key character such as Holly, either at the end of the book or part way through.
- Working as a class, produce a role-on-the-wall of Holly. Display it alongside Varjak and draw arrows between the two roles, with words describing what the characters think of each other at a particular point in the story.
- Read the sequel **The Outlaw Varjak Paw** by **S. F. Said** and record how Varjak's character continues to develop.

Adaptations for distance learning

- In preparation for a live session, children make a note of words and phrases describing Varjak's appearance and character up to the end of Chapter 7 and their opinion of him. During the live session create an on-screen role-on-the-wall for Varjak.
- Either role play the voice of Jalal in the same way as previously described or write a letter from Jalal making the same points, but asking for a reply. Children can write their replies during independent time.

EXAMPLE 3: *DRAGON MOUNTAIN* BY KATIE AND KEVIN TSANG

Planning and resources

- Children need to be familiar with the story up to the end of Chapter 16: 'The Power of a Name.'
- Children need sight of Chapter 16 to complete the roles-on-the-wall.

You will need:

- Four role-on-the-wall outlines to represent the four main characters. These can all be the same basic outlines, differentiated by their names. Write the names of the characters in the colours of the dragons they bonded with in Chapter 16.

What to do

- Ask the children why you have written the names of the characters in different colours.
- Using the information in Chapter 16, fill the role-on-the-wall outlines with those aspects of their personalities picked out by the dragons they bonded with. e.g. Ling-Fei is wise and kind with a poet's heart.
- Children can add more characteristics to the outlines from what they have read so far and more can be added as they read the rest of the novel.

> **Reader reflections**
>
> Ask: 'Do you find it confusing or interesting to have four different dragons linked to four different children?'

Further suggestions for role-on-the-wall

Stacey de Lacey in *Oliver and the Seawigs* by Phiip Reeve.
Prince Grogbar as described in Chapter 13 and/or Granny Regurgita in Chapter 3 in *The Nothing to See Here Hotel* by Steven Butler.
Crowky in *Land of Roar* and/or *Return to Roar* by Jenny McLachlan.
Malkin in *Cogheart* and/or *Shadowsea* by Peter Bunzl.
Characters like Aada, Griete and Juan in *Ship of Shadows* by Maria Kuzniar.
Chets, Katja, Big Mak and Adrianne in *Crater Lake* by Jennifer Killick.
Compare the characters of Blue Wing and Maple in *The Shark Caller* by Zillah Bethell.
Compare how opinions about the Bird Man in *Why the Whales Came* by Michael Morpurgo may be different at the beginning of the story to opinions of him the end.

Variations on hot-seating

If children are new to hot-seating it may be best to model the process first by sitting in the hot-seat yourself. This will act as a good model for the integrity of a role and give you more confidence in the outcome. However this needs to be set up beforehand by asking the class to accept that you could represent the character. It's helpful to use a simple item of clothing such as a scarf or shawl to indicate that you are in role, as well as sitting in the chair. Using the words '*action*' and '*freeze*' to start and stop the hot-seating is also helpful. Before you sit in the hot-seat, allow time for children to devise appropriate questions and allocate one or two children to ask the first questions, so it starts smoothly. You can also agree how children will indicate they want to ask subsequent questions e.g. raising a hand.

Characters in the hot-seat can include animals and other creatures found in information texts as well as stories. The following books provide good models for questioning creatures: ***Interview with a Shark: And Other Ocean Giants Too*** and ***Interview with a Tiger: And Other Clawed Beasts Too*** by Andy Seed.

Hot-seating version 1:

An individual child or a teacher represents a character.

Planning and resources

- Decide on the objective of the hot-seating.
- Select a character and the point in the text when that character will be questioned.
- Decide how the children will be supported to devise and ask questions.

Exploring characters

You will need:

- A space at the front of the class with a chair for the hot-seat.
- A simple item of clothing such as a scarf, to represent the character.
- A few pre-prepared questions on cards if necessary.

What to do

Version 1:

- Explain the hot-seating strategy and how it will help find out more about a character and the story.
- Name the character to be in the hot-seat and introduce the clothing as a sign of role.
- Ask the children what they already know about the character from the text and record and display their responses if necessary.
- Discuss what information the character might possess in relation to the story and support the children to devise appropriate questions. This might be a general discussion followed by time to note questions down or pre-prepared questions to start them off.
- Agree on signs for when the hot-seating will start and stop and agree on how it will proceed in terms of asking and answering questions.
- If you intend to work as teacher-in-role, ask the class to accept you in role as the character for the duration of the hot-seating.
- Select children to ask the first two questions to start off the process, but make it clear that others need to ask questions after that.
- The hot-seating should last until you have achieved your objective or until the class lose interest. If you are working as teacher-in-role, concentrate on presenting an attitude rather than giving a performance. Try not to behave in a manner that is vastly different from how you would normally speak and react, as this can make it difficult for children to take the exercise seriously.
- After the hot-seating allow children a short time in pairs to summarise what they have discovered.
- Take feedback and use this as a basis for discussion.
- Once children understand the concept of hot-seating, they can work in small groups to hot-seat one of their group in a similar way to previously described.

For Versions 2–5, proceed as in Version 1 with the following adaptations:

Version 2: hot-seat on the phone

- Children work in pairs. One child plays the character at a point in the story where there is a problem to solve. The other child plays an interested role such as a friend or neighbour or remains as themselves.
- The pair sit back to back as if on the phone to each other. They take turns to speak: the character speaks first to reveal a problem, followed by the listener then offering advice.
- Pairs report back to the class on what has been advised.
- This can be adapted so the listener asks questions instead of offering advice.

Version 3: a pair or small group of children represent one character

- A pair or small group of children represent the character when sitting on chairs in the hot-seating space.
- When one of the hot-seated group speaks, they represent the voice of that character. Make it clear that members of this group should not contradict each other in terms of factual information. Usually the first statement is the one that should be accepted.
- Select a child to ask the first question, then chair the hot-seating to share out the rest of the questions and ensure each member of the hot-seated group has an opportunity to respond.
- If members of the hot-seated group appear to differ in their responses as the character, stop the process and use this as an opportunity to ask the class how they think the character would respond. The final response will need to be negotiated, with the proviso that other responses may be as valid.

Version 4: A group of children represent people associated with the central character

- Select a role for the hot-seated group as people who know something about the central character. These can be relatives, friends, fellow pupils or colleagues, teachers, neighbours or eyewitnesses to an event involving the character.
- Before starting the hot-seating, children work in pairs to consider what this group might know and feel about the main character. Encourage older or more confident children to consult the text.
- Select a child to ask the first question. Then chair the hot-seating to ensure children ask relevant questions and every person in the hot-seat has an opportunity to answer.

Version 5: half the class hot-seat the other half

- Select a large group of people linked to your text who would have some information about or interest in the central character or narrative event e.g. residents in a particular area, town councillors, neighbours, peer groups, colleagues, teachers, the police, social workers, historians or private investigators, servants in a large house or the staff of an institution.
- Arrange the chairs so that one half of the class can see the other half. This can usually be accommodated by asking children to turn chairs round rather than moving other furniture.
- Half the class will take on the roles of reporters or people seeking information, and the other half will take on the chosen roles as earlier. Explain that the reporters will hot-seat the other half as a whole group.
- Make it clear that you will take on the role of chairperson for this process.
- Before starting the hot-seating, allow the reporters time to work in pairs to prepare what they will ask and allow the other group time in pairs or threes to invent and decide what information they possess about the character or event under interrogation.

- Chair the hot-seating to ensure all children who wish to speak are given the opportunity.
- Stop the hot-seating when enough information has been revealed about the character or event under discussion.
- Work with the class to recall and record the information obtained.

Version 6: teacher-in-role hot-seats the whole class

- The whole class play the roles of eye witnesses to an event or events in a story. They are hot-seated by the teacher-in-role as another character who needs or wants information such as a journalist.
- Ask the class to accept you in role as the person who needs information.
- Make sure you maintain the role throughout the hot-seating. Ask questions that encourage the children to retell the story or events. You can purposely misunderstand things, so the children have to clarify any issues.
- This version of hot-seating can be set in the context of an imaginary online meeting or in an imaginary venue.

> **Reader reflections**
>
> Hot-seat an individual or a group of children as **readers** of your chosen text. Ask the other children to compose questions to discover what the Readers thought about the different characters, events and themes in the story. After the hot-seating, ask those who asked the questions if they shared similar responses with the Readers in the hot-seat.

Adaptations for distance learning

Version 1 can take place during a live distance learning session.

For a pre-recorded session, record yourself in role as someone who knows the character, as in Version 4. This should be a monologue as you talk about what you know and think of the character. When it's played to the children, they can make notes about what your monologue reveals about the character.

EXAMPLE 1: *FANTASTIC MR FOX* BY ROALD DAHL

What to do

Proceed as in Version 1 with the following adaptations:

- Use teacher-in-role to sit in the hot-seat as Badger to find out what he thought of Mr. Fox at the end of the story. Make it clear that you will not dress up as Badger but will use the scarf to indicate you are in role, so the children will need to be *very good at pretending*.

- Before the hot-seating, ask the children to predict what Badger might say.
- Help the children devise a couple of appropriate questions e.g. *'Did you think Mr. Fox would help you when you first met him? Were you annoyed with Mr. Fox for causing problems with the farmers?'*
- Share out these questions, but make it clear that others can ask different questions. Remind the children to listen to Badger's answers to find out if their predictions were correct.
- During the hot-seating try to reveal Badger's perspective on the events in the story, including his doubts in chapter 14, as well as his feelings for Mr. Fox. If children don't ask questions to enable that, then volunteer the information.
- After the hot-seating, discuss if the children's predictions were correct and talk about what Mr. Fox might have thought about Badger.
- Reflect on the arguments Mr. Fox put to Badger in Chapter 14, about why it was Ok to steal for food.

Extension activities

- Create roles-on-the-wall for Badger and Mr. Fox. Then join the two outlines with words along arrows to indicate their friendship/relationship.
- Children write Badger's diary, recording the moment in Chapter 14 when he challenged Mr. Fox about stealing and then accepted Mr. Fox's view.

Adaptations for distance learning

During a live session, tell the children they will be hot-seating you in role as Badger to find out what he thought of Mr. Fox. Ask the children to predict what Badger will say. Help children devise questions to find out and allocate these to individual children.

Carry out the hot-seating as in Version 1.

EXAMPLE 2: *THE HIGHWAYMAN* BY ALFRED NOYES

What to do

- Begin with **Version 1**. Use teacher-in-role to play the part of a neighbour or friend of Tim the Ostler to discover more about him. Set the hot-seating at the end of the poem. Through answers to the children's questions, present Tim's view that the Highwayman was a wicked thief, who would have got Bess into trouble if he hadn't intervened.
- Move to **Version 3**. Ask a group to be hot-seated as the villagers who frequented the inn. Discuss what this group may know and think about the deaths at the end of the poem and what questions might bring out this information.

Exploring characters

- Look at authorial intent in the way the poem is biased against Tim via the words chosen by Alfred Noyes and the impact of Charles Keeping's illustration if you have that version.
- Explore what would happen if the words describing Tim were more positive and if so, what would they be? Ask *'How would this change the story? Would it be more or less interesting?'*

Extension activities

- Write the story from Tim's perspective, either in diary form or as a letter to a friend.
- Create a role-on-the-wall version of Tim.

Adaptations for distance learning

Tell the children you will be hot-seated as Tim's neighbour during a forthcoming live session. Talk about what information a neighbour might be able to provide and ask the children to prepare questions in advance. Proceed as in Version 1.

EXAMPLE 3: *THE RASCALLY CAKE* BY JEANNE WILLIS AND KORKY PAUL

This works best with Years 2/3

What to do

- Read the story to the children.
- Ask them all to be hot-seated as neighbours of Mr. Rufus Skumskins O'Parsley, who know what he was like and what sort of cake he made.
- Ask them to accept you in role as the journalist pictured towards the end of the book, seeking more information about a huge horrible cake that is rumoured to be wandering around. There is no mention of a journalist in the text, but there is an illustration of a reporter interviewing Mr. Rufus Skumskins O'Parsley towards the end of the book.
- In role as the journalist, ask the children to tell you what happened, so they retell the story. Ask about anything not explained clearly.

The character circle

Children in role as characters discuss their relationship with the main character.

Planning and resources

- Select a text with several characters and a main protagonist. This can be part of a longer text or the whole text.

- Select a given point in the story to explore relationships between the characters. Children need to be familiar with events leading up to whatever point you select.
- Make name cards for the characters in the story, including the main character.
- Every child will need access to the text.

You will need:

- A space large enough for children to sit in a circle or semicircle.
- A name label for each character.

What to do

- Ask children to sit in a circle or semicircle and place a chair in the centre of the circle with the main character's name label on it.
- Allocate all the other characters to individual children or groups, along with their name labels.
- Refer to the text at the given point in the storyline and explain that this activity is about what the other characters thought about the main character at that point.
- Make it clear that the characters' thoughts and opinions must be based on what the children have read so far in the story.
- The children or groups playing the characters decide what their character thinks about the main character at that point in the story and why. They should aim to express this in a few sentences, which can be written down if appropriate.
- After giving children time to think, take turns round the circle, inviting each character (or a designated speaker from each character group) to say what they think of the main character at that point in the story. They should speak in role as if they were that character starting with the words *I think*.
- Then ask the class what the main character might think of the character who has just spoken.

Reader reflections

Ask: 'What do you as readers, think of the main character at this point in the story?'

Extension activity

Draw a circle in the centre of a large sheet of paper. Write the name of the main character in the circle and the name of the other characters around it.

Draw lines from each of the characters to the circle, as in a spider's web.

With suggestions from the children, write key words to describe the way each character feels about the main character along each line, with an arrow pointing towards the main character. Then using a different colour, write key words describing how the main character feels about each of the other characters.

Adaptations for distance learning

Select a text and allocate characters in the same way as earlier.

Children complete the prepared statements about the main character in written form, prior to a live online session. Ask children to make a character label to wear, or hold up when it's their turn to speak about the main character.

EXAMPLE 1: *THE DRAGON SITTER'S SURPRISE* BY JOSH LACEY

Planning and resources

Proceed as previously described, with the following adaptations:

You will need:

- A copy of the text to read aloud.
- A large name card saying *Twinkle: The Yellow Phoenix*.
- Adhesive labels for the following characters: Dragons, Mum, Gordon, Emily, Uncle Morton.

What to do

- Read the story up to the end of the letter from Uncle Morton Pickle, sent on 22 July, informing Edward that he would like to see the seven dragons when he can get out of hospital.
- Arrange the children into five groups, one for each character and choose one child from each group to wear the name label. The dragons are represented by one single group.
- Give groups time to think about what their character thinks of Twinkle and encourage them to think of and/or write down a couple of sentences that will express these thoughts. Stress that the thoughts must fit with what they know of the story so far.
- Ask one child from each character group to share what they think of Twinkle. They should talk as if they were that character but can ask advice from their group if necessary.
- Then look at the text for clues about what Twinkle thinks of the dragons, Emily, Mum, Gordon and Edward.

> ### Extension activity
>
> - Write a letter to the council from Mr. Braithwaite the neighbour, complaining about the dragons.
> - Ask the children to work in pairs or threes to improvise a conversation between local children talking about the dragons living nearby. Before they begin their improvisations, check with the text to remind them what the dragons did. Then walk around the groups in role as a passer-by, freezing the action at various points to summarise what you have overheard (see Spotlighting).
> - Use teacher-in-role to play a new neighbour who has just moved into the street and wants to know what is going on.

> **Reader reflections**
>
> Ask: *'What do you think of Twinkle at this point in the story?'*

EXAMPLE 2: *HOLES* BY LOUIS SACHER

Proceed as described in the overview, with the following adaptations:

Planning and resources

- Children need to be familiar with the text up to the end of Chapter 32.
- Allocate the following characters to individuals or groups of children: Warden; Mr. Sir; Mr. Pendanski; Zero; X-ray; Zigzag; Magnet; Armpit. All children should be given one of these roles. In large classes, some groups will have the same character.

You will need:

- Adhesive name cards for each character or stand up cards if groups are representing the characters.

What to do

- Allocate characters to individual children or groups, along with appropriate name labels.
- Ask the children to decide what their character thinks about Stanley. Arrange the class in a circle with a chair and name card representing Stanley in the middle.
- Go around the characters in turn asking one child to speak as if they were their character. Ask them what they think of Stanley and ask the class what Stanley thinks of them each time.

Alternative Version

A confident child may be able to play the part of Stanley, to express what he thinks of all or some of the characters each time.

> **Reader reflections**
>
> Ask:
>
> - *'Which characters do you like the most and why?'*
> - *'Which characters do you dislike the most and why?'*

Exploring characters 141

- 'What do you think of Stanley?'
- 'How important are a reader's feelings for the main character when reading a story? Do authors always try to make the main character likeable from the start of a story?'

Look at the character of Hector in **The Night Bus Hero** (Rauf. O.) as an example of a main character whose initial behaviour may make many readers dislike or disapprove of him.

Spotlighting/overheard conversations

This strategy allows children to improvise spontaneously on a set topic, with the class listening in to just a short snippet of that improvisation. The initial improvisation can be polished and scripted as an option.

Planning and resources

- Select a moment from a story when a character could potentially pass along a route inhabited by those who might have an opinion about them. For example neighbours in a street near where the characters live or an environment with animal or magical characters who've been watching the character.

You will need:

- A scarf or other item as a sign of role for the main character.

What to do

Introduction

- Organise the children into pairs or small groups and ask them to play the roles of those making a comment about the character in the story as that character passes by. Set the scene where the children are in role as eye witnesses to the events, either real groups from the story or imagined. When the improvisation starts, they are sitting near an open window gossiping about the character, not realising the character can hear as they pass by.
- Discuss what kind of comments might be made by these groups.
- Give the children a few minutes to think in silence about what they might say in their conversations. Stress that everyone in the group must be given the chance to say something. If a child is reluctant to speak, then ask them to participate in another way by reacting to others. If necessary make it clear that this is a school improvisation with the usual rules applying, such as keeping in line with school values.

(Optional) Polished Improvisation

- On the word *'action'* bring the conversations to life for a few minutes as a rehearsal. These should happen at the same time, so no-one group is performing to another.
- Ask groups to select and practise the best moments from the spontaneous conversations they have just had, to perform a more polished improvisation.

Spotlighting

- Explain the spotlighting strategy: When the teacher shines an imaginary spotlight over a group, that group comes to life so everyone can listen in to part of their conversation. Groups should freeze when the spotlight moves away. Groups should be silent when not in the spotlight.
- Explain that the character will walk up to each group in turn and stop. This will be a signal for that group to be in the spotlight and perform their conversations. They should start their conversation when you say *'action'* and stop on the word *'freeze.'*
- Use an item of clothing as a sign of teacher-in-role.
- Keep control of the length of time for each group to be in the spotlight. Just a minute is fine but try to ensure every child has spoken. It is not necessary to hear the full conversation each time. It's often more effective to freeze a conversation at a key point, so you can repeat a particularly salient point or summarise the comments before moving on to the next group.
- After the spotlighting discuss and record what the activity has revealed about the character or those gossiping about them. Then check this with the text to see if the children thought their conversations were accurate.

> **Extension activity**
>
> Individual children refine and write a scripted version of their group's improvised conversation.

EXAMPLE 1: *GOODNIGHT MISTER TOM* BY MICHELL MAGORIAN

Proceed as previously described, with the following adaptations:

Planning and resources

- Children should be familiar with and have sight of the text up to the end of Chapter 3, when William Beech has just accompanied Mister Tom to the shop and met with some reaction from the locals.
- Set up the space so a character can walk around groups.

Exploring characters

You will need:

- A plain woollen scarf that could have been worn by William Beech.

What to do

- Introduce the spotlighting in the context of William and Tom's visit to the shop at the end of Chapter 3.
- Ask the children to play the roles of neighbours talking about William and Tom as they pass by their windows or in the street.
- Discuss the different reactions to William and the other evacuees, based on the text up to Chapter 3. You may want to allocate different attitudes to certain groups, to ensure a balance of responses as reflected in the text.
- Using the scarf as a sign of role, play the part of William Beech as you walk down the street and overhear the conversations. Ask the children to imagine that Mr. Tom is also there.
- Proceed with the spotlighting using this context.
- After the activity, reflect on the different perspectives of the villagers and why they might have these perceptions. Talk about how these perceptions might impact on William and Tom.
- Link to information texts about real life evacuees and their hosts.

Extension activities

- Children write the villagers' comments as individual scripted pieces.
- Work with the class to record elements of the comments as a composite poem.

EXAMPLE 2: *THE BOY WHO FOOLED THE WORLD* BY LISA THOMPSON

Proceed as in the overview, with the following adaptations:

Planning and resources

- Children should be familiar with the story up to and including Chapter 18 ('In the Newspaper') when Cole's fellow pupils are staring at him after having read the newspaper article.
- Set up the space so a character can walk around groups.

You will need:

- A school tie or other item representing a school uniform as worn by Cole.

What to do

- Introduce the spotlighting in the context of Cole's fellow pupils as they walk to assembly. They are talking in groups about the newspaper article and what they think of Cole, as he pushes past them to sit in the hall. Include some of the named characters in the groups talking about Cole, like Mason and Isla.
- Discuss different reactions to the newspaper article before the spotlighting.
- After the spotlighting, reflect on the different views that have been revealed and discuss what Cole could do about the situation.

The line-up

The line-up is a powerful, interactive way to engage children in discussions about the characters and where they all fit within a story. It's also a useful way to focus on more minor characters. Children representing characters are organised by the class into a line, to form a continuum from high to low, according to a given criteria.

Planning and resources

- Children need to be familiar with the text before the activity and have access to it during the activity.

You will need:

- Space for a group of children to stand in a line at the front of the class.
- An adhesive name label for each character.

What to do

- Choose some children to represent the characters in the text and wear the name labels.
- Ask the characters to stand in a line at the front of the class in any order.
- Set the line as a continuum from highest to lowest or from one to ten with one being the lowest.
- Ask the class to suggest how to re-arrange the characters on the continuum according to a given criteria such as how kind or brave they are. Set this at a given point in the story. Different points in the story and different criteria produce different line-ups.
- You can invite various individual children to line up the characters or negotiate the order as a class. Whatever method you choose, insist on reference to the text for any final decisions.

Further Suggestions

- Invite individual children to line up the characters according to those they like the most and the least and explain why.

Exploring characters

- Invite the children representing the characters to line up according to a given criteria and ask the class if they agree or disagree.
- Lines up the characters yourself and asks the children to guess your criteria from a given list.

EXAMPLE: *THE GIRL WHO STOLE AN ELEPHANT* BY NIZRANA FAROOK

Proceed as previously described, with the following adaptations:

- Children need to be familiar with the story up to the end of Chapter 7 when Neel has been arrested.
- Ask the children to name all the characters in the story so far and write name cards for each of them.
- Give the name cards to some children and ask them to stand in a line in front of the class, holding their cards so everyone can see who they are.
- Talk about the meaning of the word *status* and how it can affect how people talk, move and behave towards others e.g. a king and a servant. Talk about the concept of a pecking order.
- Invite the class to re-arrange the line so the character with the most status in the kingdom of Serendib stands at one end and the character with the least status stands at the other. Then ask them to arrange the other characters according to where they stand in the pecking order. The purpose is to initiate discussion rather than producing an accurate line-up.
- Use this as an opportunity to discuss the minor characters in more depth.
- Repeat this activity at the end of the story to reveal how Chaya's status is now elevated to that of a hero and General Siri's status is lessened.

8 Arguments, dilemmas and debates

LINKS TO READING FOR MEANING: engaging with texts; dialogues; dilemmas and balanced arguments; characters' thoughts and feelings; different perspectives; empathy; conversations about books; justifying opinions about books.

Rationale

This chapter focuses on how drama strategies can help children explore arguments, dilemmas and debates. It includes strategies that add a physical dimension to balanced arguments and the exploration of dilemmas in texts. The activities involve the whole class and encourage children to formulate and express their own opinions on the issues in the texts. They also include whole group drama where children take part in imaginary debates and trials of characters.

Contents	
Arguments and opinions	146
Dialogue for a dilemma	150
Debates and trials	152

Drama strategies

Communal voice
Conscience alley/forest
Where do you stand now?
Whole group drama

Arguments and opinions

Conscience alley/forest

Conscience Alley is where a character walks between two lines of children, who call out different sides of an argument as the character passes. It's one of the most well-known drama strategies but is sometimes overlooked due to the need for a large space to make the alleyway. However it can be adapted to become a Conscience Forest, where the character walks around desks in a classroom to hear the comments as if they were walking around trees in a forest.

Planning and resources

- Choose a text with two clear differences of opinion or arguments.
- Make a list of the arguments in the text.
- Children need shared access to the text.

You will need:

- Two different colours to underline/ highlight the two different arguments.
- A space big enough for two lines of children to make the alleyway or space for a character to walk around the other children, as if in a forest.
- A scarf or small item of clothing to represent the character.

What to do

- Explain the activity of conscience alley or forest.
- Read the text and work with the class to highlight the two opposing arguments or points of view.
- If appropriate, discuss any opposing points of view that could be linked.
- Divide the class into two, giving each side one set of arguments to express.
- Working in pairs, give children time to decide what they will say to convince the character of their given side of the argument. In large classes, pairs will repeat the same points.
- Decide the path of the character; whether they will walk down an alleyway or around trees in a forest. If they walk down an alley then decide if they walk down one side at a time, or walk down the middle to hear alternate arguments.
- Use a curved shaped alleyway or a conscience forest with lively classes, so they can see each other easier and feel part of the action.
- Set up the character using the item of clothing as a sign of role. This can be a child or yourself as teacher-in-role.
- Make it clear that the children only speak when the character passes them. If children are new to this approach it may be best to take on the role of the character yourself, so you can moderate the pace.
- Use the words '*action*' and '*freeze*' to start and stop the drama at any point.
- Encourage children to express their views with conviction, as if they really were trying to persuade someone.
- It may be useful to repeat a few significant phrases as you walk, or pause the drama to summarise, especially if some children speak quietly.
- After the activity read further into a text to discover what decision a character finally made if this is appropriate to the story.

- If children have been allocated a point of view on an issue which may not be their own, make the two lines again and ask them to stand on the side that represents their own point of view.
- Alternatively use the following **'where do you stand now?'** activity to represent the children's own opinions. If you have a clear question relating to the issue that has a Yes/No answer, place a Yes card at one end of the room and a No card at the other. On the word GO, children walk to the area representing where they stand concerning the argument or issue. Those who are unable to decide or have mixed feelings should stand in the middle. Children are asked to explain in more detail why they are standing in a particular area. Alternatively you can use AGREE/ DISAGREE cards or a few cards with particular viewpoints written on them dotted around the room.

EXAMPLE 1: *HOLES* BY LOUIS SACHER

Proceed as previously described, with the following adaptations:

Planning, resources and what to do

- Children need to be familiar with the story up to the point of Stanley's *find* in Chapter 13.
- Use conscience alley to represent the choice Stanley has to make about what he should do with his *find*.
- The voices along the alley will represent Stanley's thoughts as he grapples with this decision.
- Help children to separate Stanley's thoughts into two sides: one side represents reasons for giving the find to either Mr. Pendanski or the Warden and the other side represents giving it to X-ray. The third option of keeping the find is dismissed by Stanley very quickly, so would not be part of the decision, unless the children feel it should be. If so, this can be accommodated by a small turn in the alley at the start of his journey.
- Divide the children into two groups to represent the two arguments and allow them time to plan and rehearse what they will say when Stanley passes. This usually works better in pairs. Children can decide how they want to organise this. They could say the words in chorus, speak the same words one after the other or share out the words, but all children should be encouraged to say something.
- Select a child to walk slowly down the middle of the alley in role as Stanley or play the role yourself.
- At the end of the activity, read the rest of Chapter 13 revealing what happened next.

EXAMPLE 2: *THE WRECK OF THE ZANZIBAR* BY MICHAEL MORPURGO

Proceed as in Example 1, with the following adaptations:

Planning and resources

- Children should be familiar with the story of The Wreck Of The Zanzibar up to and including the diary entry for Sept 8th up to the line *'I should tell him, I know I should.'*

You will need:

- An upturned basket or similar object to represent the turtle.

What to do

- Read to where Laura says *'I should tell him, I know I should.'*
- Discuss the dilemma in Laura's mind over whether she should tell her starving family she has discovered an upturned turtle, or keep it secret and try to rescue it.
- Divide the class into two groups to make the conscience alley. One group should give reasons why Laura should save the turtle and the other group should give reasons why it should not be saved.
- Place an upturned basket or other item to represent the turtle at the end of the alley and choose one child to play Laura as she walks through conscience alley, listening to both sides.
- Repeat, asking children to develop their use of appropriate expression and tone of voice to match their given viewpoint.
- At the end, ask the child playing Laura what decision she would take based on these arguments.
- Then ask the rest of the children what decision they would take if they were Laura.
- Read the last few lines of this day's entry to discover what Laura decided to do in the story.

> ### Reader reflections
>
> Ask the children, *'As readers did you find Laura's dilemma interesting or frustrating or did you have another reaction?'*
>
> After reading the rest of the book ask: *'Why do you think Michael Morpurgo wanted Laura to save the turtle?'*

EXAMPLE 3: CONSCIENCE FOREST AS A DREAM

Texts:

The Pied Piper of Hamelin **by Robert Browning, illustrated by Kate Greenaway**
The Pied Piper of Hamelin **by Robert Browning illustrated by Arthur Rackham**

Proceed as in the previous examples, with the following adaptations:

Planning and resources

- Children need to be familiar with the story before the activity.

What to do

- Explain that the activity will show the Mayor walking through a forest during a dream, on the night before he made his decision not to pay the Pied Piper.
- In preparation, help the children list the arguments for and against not paying the Piper that might have been going through the Mayor's mind e.g. *'The rats would probably have gone anyway, so the Pied Piper didn't do anything to deserve the money/there are no more rats so why should we pay?/the money can be spent on the town/people will be angry if I give away the town's money/the people will be angry if I don't keep my word/ it's not right to break a promise/the Pied Piper might come back and threaten the town if I don't pay him/he is only one person, what harm can he do us?'* etc.
- Allocate different points of view to different children and ask them to call out the thoughts when you pass by in role as the Mayor. Weave in and out as if in the forest, allowing some children to repeat their thoughts to convey a dream-like effect.

Reader reflections

Use '**where do you stand now?'** to ask the following two questions:

- *'Was the mayor right not to pay the Pied Piper? YES or NO?'*
- *'Who is to blame for the disappearance of the children or is there shared blame?'* Write name cards as the children suggest those who might share the blame (likely to be the mayor and the Piper, but add the rats if they are not suggested) and place them around the room before asking 'where do you stand now?'
- If you have been reading all or part of the poem, ask: *'Does the poem give us any clues as to who Robert Browning thinks is to blame?'*

Dialogue for a dilemma

This activity uses the communal voice drama strategy to create an imaginary conversation between two characters about a dilemma in a text. The conversation is represented by different children who take turns to speak on behalf of the characters. It can also be adapted to speculate on possible conversations *off camera* that do not appear in the text.

Planning and resources

- Select a moment from a text with a dilemma or a likely *off camera* conversation, involving two characters.
- Children need to be familiar with the story in the text up to the point of the conversation.

You will need:

- A cleared performance space with two chairs placed at opposite ends. This can be at the front of a classroom or in a larger space with children standing in a circle to create the performance space.
- One object or item as a prop, if appropriate for the story.

What to do

- Invite the children to speculate about the forthcoming conversation between the two characters in the story and predict what the outcome might be.
- Ask two children to represent the characters in the performance space by sitting on the chairs.
- Ask the class to describe how each of the characters would be positioned: their stance, position and body shape. Once agreed, ask the characters to take up these positions during the conversation.
- Ask the class which character would be the first to speak and what they would say. Ask the child giving the first suggestion to stand behind this character and say the line as if they were that character's voice.
- Ask for a volunteer to stand behind the other character to voice their response.
- Keep asking *What would be said next?* to encourage different children to stand behind the characters to keep the dialogue going.
- If space is limited, the 'voices' can return to the audience after speaking. In a larger space they can remain sitting or standing behind or around the characters
- Carry on in this manner until the point where you and the children feel the conversation should or would end. If children are repeating phrases, pause the drama to discuss how to improve it.
- Stop the drama and read what happened next in the text.

Reader reflections

Ask the children whether their version of the conversation would make a good addition to the story and why?

Extension activity

Children develop and write their improvised version of the conversation as a script or as part of a graphic novel with speech bubbles.

EXAMPLE: *THE FIREWORK MAKER'S DAUGHTER* BY PHILIP PULLMAN

Proceed as previously described, with the following adaptations:

Ages 7-11 (Years 2-6)

Planning and resources

- Children should be familiar with the story up to the part in Chapter 2 where Lila tells Chulak she intends to leave home to find the secrets of firework making.

You will need:

- A cleared space with two chairs opposite each other.
- Adhesive name labels for Chulak and Lila.

What to do

- Read up to the line in Chapter 2 when Chulak says *No! Wait! You ought to talk to him* . . .
- Work with the class to record Lila's and Chulak's main arguments for and against Lila's decision to leave.
- Use communal voice to create a conversation where Chulak tries to persuade Lila to stay. Encourage the children to use the arguments as a prompt, aiming to make the conversation realistic and interesting to the reader, as if they were the author.
- Stop the drama and read the rest of Chapter 2 to find out what the author decided Lila should do.

Reader reflections

- Ask the children whether they think a longer conversation between Chulak and Lila would have made the story more or less interesting. Talk about why they think the author chose to move straight to the line *'But Lila wouldn't listen.'*
- Use the **'where do you stand now?'** strategy with **yes/no** cards to ask the children whether they would have included a longer conversation at this point if they were Philip Pullman. Sometimes children like to do this again, as they may change their minds after listening to others.

Debates and trials

Imaginary debates

- All the children in a class are allocated a point of view in advance of an imaginary debate, so they are debating in role. However when the imaginary debate is over, it's important to give all the children an opportunity to voice their own opinions rather than those they have been allocated in the drama.
- Children need to read information texts or stories in preparation for the debate.
- You can use teacher-in-role to chair the debate or role-play a witness for one side, with another adult or a confident child playing a witness for the other side to spark the debate.

Characters on Trial

- Debates can also take the form of imaginary court trials, with some children taking on the role of the jury. They make the final decision of guilty or not guilty after listening to arguments for and against the character's actions. The arguments can be discussed as a class prior to the trial and then presented by individuals or groups of children who feel confident in these roles. Adopting formal court language and roles adds authenticity to the drama. An imaginary trial works well with familiar bad characters such as the Wolf or a Giant in a fairy tale, but can work with other characters from novels or narrative poems where responsibility for an event is not clear cut, such as the part Tim played in the death of **The Highwayman by Alfred Noyes**.
- Link to other books about characters on trial such as: **The Trial of the Big Bad Wolf by Liam Farrell.**

9 Settings, atmosphere and suspense

LINKS TO READING FOR MEANING: engaging with texts; recall; vocabulary; interpreting meaning; exploring settings, mood and atmosphere; exploring suspense; authorial intent; justifying opinions on texts.

Rationale

This chapter explores how imagined observations, sounds and key words can engage children with settings and suspense in stories.

Contents	
Exploring a setting	155
Sounds for words	159
Characters as sounds	161
A Dreamy text	162
Tracking the suspense	165

Drama strategies

Dreamscapes
Guided tour
Pathway
Role-on-the-wall
Sound effects
Soundscapes
Suspense alley
Visualisation/the object game

DOI: 10.4324/9781003250777-12

Exploring a setting

Planning

- Select a text with a strong visual setting.
- Plan to use the object game with stories set in smaller indoor spaces.
- Plan to use the guided tour with settings you could travel through like a landscape, street, park or town.

Resources

For the object game you will need:

- A text extract with a setting containing objects, creatures or defined physical features.
- A small performance space in the classroom.
- Highlighted key words in the text describing the setting.
- Access to the highlighted text for all children.

For the guided tour you will need:

- (Optional) Copies of a map or illustrations relating to the setting and/or tape to mark out areas on the floor.
- Sight of the text for all children.
- One A4 sheet of plain paper and a pencil for each child (for the paired work option).
- A hall or cleared space.

What to do

The object game

- Ask the children to stand in a circle or sit within view of a small performance space.
- Read the text extract describing the setting.
- Select an item from the setting without telling the children what you have chosen and stand in the space.
- Without naming it, describes yourself as if you were that item and ask the class to guess what item from the setting you are representing. Add a mimed action if your chosen item has movement, such as a tree swaying or a door blowing back and forth.
- When children have guessed the item, ask them to describe what that item may have witnessed in the story.
- Ask the children why they think the author placed this item in the setting, both in terms of the storyline and the mood or atmosphere it creates for the reader.
- Working in pairs, ask children to select another item from the setting and prepare an un-named written description in role as that item, along with actions if appropriate.
- Repeat the game with pairs of children describing themselves in role as the items for the rest of the class to guess. Pairs can decide which of them reads out their description, but both should perform any actions.

The guided tour

Version 1: whole class walk through

- Read a description of the setting from the text. Ask the children to pretend you are going to take them on an imaginary guided tour of this setting.
- Depending on the needs of the children it may be useful to mark out areas from the setting on the floor with masking tape.
- Invite the children to follow you in crocodile formation as you lead the way through the setting and narrate the experience. Freeze the action at various points to ask the children what they might see or sense and how they might feel at that point.
- You can adapt the hall activity to the classroom by asking the children to put on imaginary headphones for an audio guide before closing their eyes to listen to your narration of the guided tour.
- Conclude by asking children to compare their responses to the setting with the responses of the characters if appropriate.

Version 2: paired work

- **In the classroom** - As you read a description of the setting to the children, ask them to close their eyes and imagine they were actually there. Then discuss what some children saw, felt, sensed etc. Link to any relevant map, plan or illustration as an interpretation/visualisation of the setting.
- Work with the children to make notes describing the setting, as if for a guided tour for visitors. Provide examples of the language and phrases often used in guided tours e.g. *'Walk along until you see,' 'If you look to your left you will see . . . and you may notice,'* etc.
- **In a hall or cleared space** - children work in pairs as A and B. Child A is a guide for child B who is a visitor.
- The guide slowly leads the visitor through the setting, describing what the visitor can see and sense as if conducting a guided tour. Encourage them to improvise by suggesting sensory experiences such as dipping their hand in a stream and warnings such as crossing a bridge with care, ducking under a low ceiling, avoiding a chair etc. Once through the setting, the pairs swap roles and re-trace their steps, maybe noticing and adding different things.

Extension activities

- Invite children to sketch an illustration of the setting based on their experience and/or write features of the experience as a written guide.
- If appropriate to the text, invite the children to compare their experiences of the setting to those of the characters in the story.

Guided tour as an outside broadcast

- Children work in pairs as journalists to prepare and then record an outside broadcast of the setting for an imaginary radio show. They give a commentary as if they are walking or travelling through the setting. This is particularly effective where there is a map or plan of a setting such as Eerie-on-Sea in **Malamander by Thomas Taylor.**

Guided tour as a pathway

- Children arrange themselves to form a pathway around the room. Working in pairs or small groups, they use their bodies to create obstacles and features of the pathway based on the setting in the text e.g. pairs joining hands to form an archway for a traveller to walk under, lying down as an obstacle to step over etc.
- The traveller who negotiates the pathway is a child in role as a visitor.
- The children decide on one thing a traveller might see and/or sense when passing along their part of the pathway and call this out as the traveller passes by.
- If appropriate, compare the traveller's experiences to those described in the setting in the story.

EXAMPLE 1: *CHARLOTTE'S WEB* BY E. B. WHITE

Proceed as in the Object Game and Version 1, with the following adaptations:

Planning and resources

- Focus on the description of the barn at the beginning of Chapter 3, 'Escape.'
- Children need to understand what barns are for and what they look like and they need to be familiar with the farm objects in the setting.
- Highlight all the objects in the barn on a copy of the text extract.
- All children will need access to the highlighted text during the activity.

You will need:

- A hall or cleared space

What to do

- Play the Object Game with items based on the highlighted text.
- Invite the children to go with you on an imaginary visit to the barn described in the text.
- Ask the children to imagine/pretend that the space they are in is the barn. Choose a place in the room to represent the '*big doors*' as an entry point into the barn. Ask them to imagine they are visiting in summer when the doors were open.
- Organise the children into a crocodile formation in pairs. Ask them to follow you quietly into the barn so as not to disturb the animals.

- Introduce the words 'action' and 'freeze' to start and stop the drama.
- On the word 'action,' lead the children quietly through the doors of the barn and gather them together in the centre. It's important you behave as if you were really there. Mention a few things you can see as you arrive, such as swallows' nests.
- Lead the children on a guided tour round the barn, based on the text e.g. point out features like the hay loft and the stalls for the work horses.
- Discover a work horse in one of the stalls and describe it. Announce your intention to stroke it. Ask the children for advice on how best to do that. Pretend to carefully stroke the horse and then ask if any of the children would like to do the same. If everyone wants to stroke a horse, you can find more horses in the stalls. Ask the children if anyone has stroked a horse before and how it felt to stroke it.
- Lead the children round the barn, pointing out the objects mentioned in the text e.g. ladders, lawn mowers etc. Ask which of these objects could be dangerous if children played with them in the barn e.g. pitch forks.
- Lead them out of the barn and stop the drama.
- Talk about the experience, asking what children felt, sensed and saw.
- Re read the text, asking them to imagine their visit. Was there anything there they missed?

Extension activities

- Children draw the inside of the barn as part of a letter to one of the characters about their visit.
- Work as a class to create a sensory version of the guided tour.

EXAMPLE 2: *THE HOBBIT* BY J. R. TOLKIEN

Proceed as in Version 2: paired work, with the following adaptations:

What to do

- Use the introductory paragraphs in Chapter 1 as the text. Following the suggestions for Version 2: paired work, ask the guides to take on the roles of estate agents, showing their partners round the Hobbit Hole as a desirable residence for a *'well-to-do'* person.
- To prepare children for the activity, talk about the comfortable aspects of the Hobbit Hole that an agent could build on e.g. clean air in the tunnel, carpets and plenty of pegs for clothes. Then talk about what we are left to imagine e.g. the inside of the rooms, especially the best rooms with views over the garden.
- Allow children time to create what they imagine the insides of the rooms might look like and plan their tours.

Extension activity

Children sketch the visuals for an imaginary estate agent's website, describing the Hobbit Hole as a desirable residence.

Further Suggestions for the Object Game and/or Guided Tours:

- **Crater Lake by Jennifer Killick**

    Crater Lake based on the description in Chapter 3.

- **The Castle of Tangled Magic by Sophie Anderson**

    The Land of Forbidden Magic described at the beginning of Chapter 12.

- **Paddington at Large by Michael Bond**

    The park in Chapter 2: Mr. Gruber's Outing.

- **Brightstorm by Vashti Hardy**

    Beggins Hall towards the end of Chapter 3.

- **Angel's Child by Larraine S Harrison**

    The cottage on the cliff in Chapter 4.

- **The Haunting of Aveline Jones by Phil Hickes**

    The sections describing Lieberman's second-hand bookshop in parts of Chapter 2.

- **The Ship Of Shadows by Maria Kuzniar**

    The ship's library in Chapter 7.
    The navigator's room at the end of Chapter 14.
    The Consul's party in Chapter 28.

- **Varjak Paw by S. F. Said**

    The descriptions of the Contessa's house in Chapter 1.

Sounds for words

Planning and resources

- Select a short text extract with a setting that has potential for sound effects.
- Highlight the words or phrases that could be expressed via sound. If appropriate include phrases creating mood as well as real life sounds.
- All children need sight of the highlighted text.

You will need:

- Percussion instruments.

What to do

- Place the instruments where children can see them.
- Read the extract to the children and ask them what they notice about the parts that are highlighted.
- Demonstrate the instruments one at a time and ask the children to consider which could be used for each highlighted part and why. Voices or other sounds could also be used.
- Agree what instruments or voices to use for each highlighted word or phrase and allocate different children to create the sounds. These can be individuals and/or groups.
- Mark the text to indicate which sounds go with which highlighted parts, so children are prepared.
- Read the extract again, stopping after each highlighted part to allow the children to make the sounds. You may need to give a sign such as raising and lowering your hand, so children know when to start and stop.
- Talk about which sound effects the children thought worked well and why and which they felt were less successful.

Extension activity

Working in pairs or groups, children highlight appropriate words and phrases to create sounds for another short extract from the same or a different text.

EXAMPLE: *THE IRON MAN* BY TED HUGHES

Proceed as previously described, with the following adaptations:

Planning and resources

- Children need to be familiar with and have sight of the first part of Chapter 1 of *The Iron Man* during the activity.

What to do

- Use the extract from the first sentence of Chapter 1 up to the words '*silent*' and '*unmoving*' on the next page.
- Highlight and provide suitable instruments for some of the words and phrases e.g. '*The wind sang through his iron fingers*' (a xylophone or glockenspiel).
- Organise children into two different groups to represent the sounds relating to the wind and the sea and give them time to practise with the instruments.

Settings, atmosphere and suspense

- Start with both the wind and sea groups making sounds together before the first line is read, to set the scene. Then read the text aloud, pausing for children to make the sounds at the appropriate moments.
- (Optional) Repeat for an audio recording to aid discussion and reflection.

Characters as sounds

Planning and resources

- Select a description of a well-defined character from a text that is familiar to the children.

You will need:

- A range of percussion instruments and any other objects to make sounds as appropriate to the text.

What to do

- Read the text extract to the children, asking them to pay close attention to the character's feelings and experiences and how the character is portrayed by the author.
- Work with the class to create a soundscape to reflect the character. Make it clear that a soundscape is a collage or collection of sounds that reflect and represent the character. It can include speaking key words from the text as well as sounds or you can record the sounds first and then add the words during a live performance.
- Children may need to experiment with different ways to create sounds with their voices, bodies and objects as well as any instruments before the activity e.g. whistling or clicking, clapping, stamping, crunching paper or scratching on a board etc. Children can make sounds individually or in groups, each choosing a different sound to reflect aspects of the character.
- The soundscape can be turned into an imaginary sound machine, which repeats the sounds on a loop until switched off. Significant words can also be repeated and overlapped for maximum impact.
- Practise and then perform the soundscape as a class conducted by yourself or a child. The conductor can instruct the children to play together or at different times to build up and release tension to reflect the changing emotions of the character.
- Making an audio recording of the activity provides an opportunity for the children to assess how well the soundscape reflects the character.

Extension activity

Older or more confident children can work in groups to produce their own soundscape for different characters. They should be asked to justify their choice of sounds. Once completed, these can be shared with the rest of the class to see if they can identify what or who they represent.

EXAMPLE 1: CROWKY IN *LAND OF ROAR* BY JENNY MCLACHLAN

Proceed as previously described, with the following adaptations:

What to do

- Children need to be familiar with the story up to and including Chapter 40 and need sight of the illustration of Crowky in that chapter.
- Draw a role-on-the-wall outline of Crowky based on the illustration of him in Chapter 40. Ask the children what this image tells the reader about Crowky. Write inside the outline what the children know about Crowky from the text and illustration. Use the words at the beginning of Chapter 40 to support the activity.
- Talk about the impact Crowky creates when he appears in the story and link to how that is reflected in the illustration in Chapter 40. Compare this illustration to the mood created in the illustration of Win jumping into the lagoon in Chapter 24. Use this as an opportunity to talk about how words and illustrations in texts work together to create meaning.
- Produce the Crowky soundscape as a whole class, adding key words from the text that express the kind of character he is and the mood he creates.

> ### Reader reflections
>
> Ask the children for their opinions on the other illustrations of Crowky in the story and why they think the illustrator chose to depict him this way. Discuss the impact of the illustrations on the reader.
>
> Ask: 'If there were no illustrations of Crowky would he seem as menacing?'
>
> Look at illustrations of menacing characters in other books the children have read and talk about how these contribute to the way readers feel about the characters.

A dreamy text

This activity is based on a dreamscape where children perform key words and phrases from the text as if they are spoken in a dream. There are several ways of doing this, but one way is to use the same context as conscience forest, where children stand as if they are trees in a forest, whispering and chanting key lines from the text. However, unlike conscience forest there is no dilemma to consider. The dreamscape focuses on the mood and atmosphere of the text with added sounds if appropriate. A dreamscape based on mood and atmosphere draws attention to how the author or poet uses words to create powerful settings that often reflect the emotions of the characters. It can also be set to music.

What to do

- Use the following example as a model for using a dreamscape with poems and stories:

EXAMPLE: DARKNESS CLOSES IN, FROM THE VERSE NOVEL LITTLE LIGHT BY CORAL RUMBLE

Planning and resources

- Children need to be familiar with this verse novel up to the poem called *Darkness Closes In*.
- Every child will need sight of the poem to prepare for the activity.
- This works best in a space big enough for the main character to weave in and out of the other children, but it can be adapted for a classroom with the children standing by or sitting at their desks to represent the voices of the trees.

What to do

- Read the poem aloud to the children and ask them to join in with the repeated line *Darkness closes in*.
- Ask them what effect the repetition of this line has and talk about what kind of mood it creates.
- Invite further discussion on the meaning by saying: 'I wonder what kind of darkness is closing in?'
- Ask them to imagine that Ava had a nightmare the night after this incident. In her dream, she was walking through a forest, feeling like real darkness was closing in on her, when suddenly the trees began to whisper words and phrases to torment her about what had happened that day.
- Invite the children to perform the dream, known as a dreamscape. Explain that in this dreamscape, someone in role as Ava will walk around the imaginary trees. The others in the class will speak the words of the whispering trees as she passes.
- Explain that during the performance, the trees will speak single words and short phrases from the poem and every now and again they will all chant the repeated line. Ask them which single words or phrases in the poem would be particularly menacing e.g. *Suspended, Mum is crying, no defence*.
- In pairs ask children to select two or three menacing words or phrases from the poem that they could learn by heart for the dreamscape. They will need to repeat these each time Ava passes by.
- Involve the children in as many decisions about the performance as possible e.g. 'When will they chant the repeated line? Should they add swaying tree-like movements when they speak? What will be the signal for the dream coming to an end? Where will Ava walk so she hears all the trees at least twice?'

- Choose a child to represent Ava or play this role yourself.
- Practise the dream sequence and then ask the children questions about how it could be improved e.g. *'Does it communicate the seriousness of the moment in the poem? Were the words spoken with expression? Were the whispered words loud and clear enough for the character and/or an audience to hear? Should the character take a different path? Did the choral speaking work? Should we add movements or did the movements work?'* etc.
- Run a final performance. If it can be recorded either on audio or video, then children can further assess the impact and whether it reflects the mood of the poem.

> **Reader reflections**
>
> Use **'where do you stand now?'** agree/disagree cards to discover the readers' views on the following statements:
>
> *'The incident would be very different if it were written as prose.'*
> *'Repeating the last line after every verse makes it really feel like darkness is closing in.'*

> **Extension activity**
>
> Compare the mood in this poem to the mood in other poems about the dark such as ***The Dark* by James Carter** from ***Weird, Wild and Wonderful***.

Further suggestions

The Lie Tree *by Frances Hardinge*

Create a dreamscape for Faith, based on the description in Chapter 20 from the line *'Faith walked through a midnight forest'* to the line *'She was not alone.'*

Fears of the Unknown *by Sue Hardy Dawson from* If I Were Other Than Myself

Create a dreamscape for an unspecified character based on the fears in this poem.

Terrible Lizards *by Sue Hardy-Dawson from* Where Zebras Go

Create a dreamscape about dinosaurs for an unspecified character, based on the words and phrases in this poem.

Tracking the suspense

This activity uses a strategy known as suspense alley, which is a version of conscience alley without the dilemma. It focuses instead on the cumulative effect of particular words and phrases that evoke suspense.

Planning and resources

- Select a short text extract that illustrates some features of suspense writing.
- Children will need to know the context of the extract and/or have read up to that part of the story and will need a copy of the extract they can highlight to prepare for the activity.
- Suspense alley works best in a cleared space where children can stand in two lines opposite each other to form an alley. The cumulative nature of suspense is best represented via walking through an alley, but it can be adapted for the classroom by asking the main character to walk around the desks.

What to do

- Read the extract to the children and talk about how suspense is built up during the reading.
- Provide one or two examples of how the author uses particular techniques to create the suspense in the extract e.g. holding back information, providing hints, using selective vocabulary to create tension or slowing down the action.
- In pairs, ask the children to highlight or identify at least 3 words or phrases that contribute to the suspense. Pair up less confident children with those who are more confident at speaking out loud.
- If appropriate, focus on the particular parts of speech such as the verbs, adjectives or adverbs in the extract that create suspense.
- Collect and record these words or phrases. Work with the children to identify any they have missed out and number them according to the order in which they appear.
- Share out the words on the list amongst the pairs. In large classes, different pairs may have the same words.
- Ask children to work with their partner to organise and practise saying their words out loud. They can either say them chorally or take turns to say different words. Encourage them to think about the meanings and say the words with appropriate expression.
- Either choose a child to represent the main character or play the part yourself.
- Organise the children to stand in two rows opposite each other to form an alley.

Version 1

- Those saying numbers one and two on the list should stand at one end of the alley and those with the higher numbers stand at the other end to reflect the build-up of suspense in the text.

166 Ages 7–11 (Years 2–6)

- As the character walks slowly down the middle of the alley, the children call out their words when the character passes them. If necessary decide which row speaks first each time.
- Repeat the process to reinforce the words.
- Talk about the cumulative effect these words have on a reader and the mood and tension they create.

Version 2

- Make the alley into a more dream-like experience with children repeating the words in any order at any time.

Extension activity

- Invite the children to turn the list of suspense words and phrases into a poem.
- Apply the same activity to create an action alley for another extract where there is a lot of action. This time focus on the verbs.

Figure 9.1 Book cover of Red Snow by Larraine S Harrison.

Settings, atmosphere and suspense 167

EXAMPLE: *RED SNOW* BY LARRAINE S HARRISON

Proceed as previously described, with the following adaptations:

What to do

- Use the extract on pages 30-31 in Chapter 3, 'Storm,' that begins with the word *'Tracks'* and ends with the words *'They were trapped.'*
- Either read the book up to this extract or provide the following summary before reading the extract:

    Megan and Ryan have been feeding a trapped and injured wild cat in some woods near their Yorkshire home, but decide to keep it secret because wild cats are an endangered species. On their way home in a storm they find evidence of a second, potentially more dangerous wildcat on the loose.

- Talk about how the author builds up the tension from the discovery of the tracks to the point where they are trapped inside a garden with the wildcat. Ask them to pick out key words that contribute to the suspense e.g. *tracks, fear, uneasy, warned, roaring wind, trespassing, shocked, red raw, gruesomely, grisly, slammed, pleaded, anxiously, worsening, violent, deep low growl, trapped.*
- Ask children to use some of these words and other phrases to call out, as a child playing Megan walks down suspense alley.
- After the activity ask the children if they feel that the conflicting attitude of the two characters adds to the tension i.e. Ryan is curious and takes risks but Megan is cautious.
- Talk about how the author's choice of an enclosed setting, the description of the *grisly* raw meat in the cages and the references to the wind and the storm all contribute to the build-up of the suspense, leading to the final moment when the pair become trapped.

    Another gust of wind slammed the gate shut
    raw meat . . . dangling from the roof . . . swaying gruesomely in the wind
    Underneath the roar of the wind . . .

Reader reflections

Ask:

- 'Did this period of suspense make you want to keep reading? If so why?'
- 'Should the author have made the period of suspense shorter or longer or was it about right? Why do you think this?'

10 Whole group drama
The inside story

LINKS TO READING FOR MEANING: emotional engagement with stories; researching information texts; empathy; identifying themes; authorial intent and viewpoints; comparisons across texts; characters' thoughts, feelings, motives and problems; different perspectives; interpreting meaning; conversations about books; justifying opinions on texts.

Rationale

This chapter looks at how whole group drama works to motivate and engage children from within the story itself, providing an imaginary experience that creates a personal relationship with, or a link to a text. It's a way of bringing children closer to the events in a text and can be a holding form within which other drama strategies are employed, to slow down the action and deepen the meaning. The activities need to be adapted to suit the particular context of your story, but most will follow the three-part whole group drama pattern of context, problem, reflection.

Content	
An overview of whole group drama	169
Dramatic play	170
An extra scene	172
Stepping into history	178
Offering advice	185
A similar story	187

Drama strategies

Actions
Freeze-frame
Improvisation
Mantle-of-the-expert
Pathway
Role-on-the-wall
Spotlighting

DOI: 10.4324/9781003250777-13

Teacher-in-role
Thought tracking
Whole group drama
Other drama strategies can be employed to enable further exploration and/or reflection within and following a whole group drama activity.

An overview of whole group drama

Planning and resources

- Decide if you want to use whole group drama to explore the actual events of your chosen text, or the theme within a similar or different context.
- Choose a collective role for the children that fits with the events of the story or sequence e.g. tourists, visitors, school children on a trip, space travellers, friends, neighbours, villagers, farm workers, safety officers, warriors, archaeologists, researchers, scientists, historians, environmentalists, inhabitants of magic lands, teachers or colleagues.
- Create a simple appropriate occupational task for the collective roles, such as preparing for a journey, working on jobs, making camp etc.
- Decide on a problem for the collective role that would enable them to explore the issues in the text. For example, the setting for a story with a theme about 'greed' could be a castle full of servants preparing for a greedy queen's birthday. The collective role for the children would be the servants, who are told to prepare vast amounts of food for the queen. The problem occurs when the servants are sent a message from the queen saying their wages are cut, so they can't buy enough food for themselves.
- If you are intending to use teacher-in-role to pose the problem, plan how and when you will use it.

It can be useful to start off by playing what is sometimes called a *shadowy* role as one of the group and then play a different role later.

- Either select an item of clothing as a sign of role if you are using teacher-in-role to pose a problem, or prepare a written message from a character to pose the problem.
- Plan to use the hall or cleared space for the start of the collective role play, or decide how to adapt it to a smaller space.

What to do

1 Establish the context

- Make a contract with the children to play the parts of the chosen collective roles in the imaginary setting and define the space for the drama.
- Introduce the words '*action*' and '*freeze*' to start and stop the drama and define where and when it will begin.
- Make it clear that even though the actions will be mimed, the children should talk as if they were really there.

- Organise children into small groups and give them time to decide what tasks they will perform in role when the drama begins. If you are in a large space suggest that the groups interact with each other for some reason such as helping each other with jobs, swapping items for things they need or buying food from each other. This gives the activity more authenticity and results in improved levels of engagement.
- Begin the drama with a whole class freeze-frame, inviting the groups to take up their positions as they start their first task. Invite children into the freeze-frame a few groups at a time, with praise for those who can hold the freeze.
- On the word '*action*,' bring the freeze to life. If you are in role as one of the big group, you can visit each small group in role to build belief. Depending on the context, you can offer to help them with their jobs, swap items for things you need or ask for advice.
- Let this run for a few minutes and then stop the drama with the word '*freeze*.'

2 Pose a problem

- Move time on by narrating that the collective roles were contacted by someone with some important information. If you are using teacher-in-role to pass on this information, make the contract to play the part and use the item of clothing as a sign.
- Restart the drama with the word '*action*' and pose the problem either via teacher-in-role or a written message.
- Discuss solutions in role if possible and enact them before stopping the drama. If the solutions are not possible to enact, then narrate a likely outcome or produce evidence e.g. letters to show how the problem was solved. If the solutions require research or a longer discussion then pause the drama to allow that to happen.

3 Reflect

- Give children an opportunity to reflect on their experiences and link to the theme and the text. Include any universal links if appropriate.

Dramatic play

Building a context for a whole group drama often involves some kind of occupational mimed actions known as dramatic play. This fosters a sense of commitment to the drama and paves the way for children to solve an associated problem or take up a challenge. However, it can be used as an activity in its own right to link children to a story. For example, children use dramatic play to create a public garden and a plaque to commemorate the events in a story. Dramatic play works well with Years 2/3 who enjoy the similarities with play. Some story settings such as hotels, gardens, workshops etc create ideal opportunities for this activity.

Use the following Example as a model for linking dramatic play to other stories:

💡 EXAMPLE: *HOTEL FLAMINGO* BY ALEX MILWAY

Planning and resources

- This works best when it takes place in a hall or cleared space to create a sense of a busy hotel.
- Children need to be familiar with the story up to the end of Chapter 5.

You will need:

- Name cards for the following: Hotel Flamingo; Madame Le Pig; Eva Koala; Stella Giraffe; Hilary Hippo.
- A note to the children from Anna and the characters, thanking them for helping in the hotel.

What to do

- Read the children the start of Chapter 6 ('The Pink Flamingos') up to and including the line *'Hotel Flamingo was full of staff. . .'*
- Ask the children to pretend they are some new staff employed to work at the hotel. Their challenge is to help the existing staff complete all the jobs to help improve it. Explain that they will be organised into groups to help the characters who are in charge of the different jobs. Bring out the character name cards and ask the children if they can remember what specific jobs these characters had, then refer to the end of Chapter 4 to check.
- Talk about what each job could involves e.g. Eva Koala will be cleaning and tidying up the restaurant and checking all the cutlery and crockery, making table displays etc.
- Either allocate groups to help the different characters, or let the children choose who they would like to help.
- Place the name of the hotel on display and ask the children to pretend that the space they are working in is the hotel. Place the character names around the room to indicate where each group will work and ask each group to sit by the name of the character they will be working for.
- Make it clear that although the children need to mime the actions for the jobs, they can talk and behave as if they were really there. Give groups time to decide on what jobs they will do and which one they will do first. They should think of a frozen position to start their first job. Tell the children that you would like to join them in the drama as someone who supplies the cleaning materials and may visit them as they work.

- Ask children to stand in their frozen positions ready to start their jobs. Bring the hotel to life on the word '*action*' and visit each group in role, asking if they need any more cleaning materials. Use this as an opportunity to ask them about their jobs and build belief in the context.
- Stop the drama and narrate that the next day the children received a letter. Read out the thank you letter from Anna and the characters.
- Read more of Chapter 6 up to the line '*This problem of guests would be a lot harder to solve, she thought.*'
- In pairs, followed by sharing with the class, ask the children for their suggestions on how Anna might attract more guests before reading to the end of Chapter 6 and beyond to find out what she decided.

Reflection

- Ask the children which job they thought was the hardest to do and which if any, they enjoyed.
- Ask if any children have visited real hotels and what jobs the staff had there. Were they similar to the jobs they helped with in the drama?

Reader reflections

Compare and contrast the Hotel Flamingo with the descriptions of another hotel in the first two chapters of **The Nothing to See Here Hotel** by **Steven Butler**. Ask the children which hotel they would prefer to stay in and why.

Extension activity

Children write a diary entry about the day they helped Anna and the characters at the Hotel Flamingo.

Further suggestions: a commemorative garden

Text: The Iron Man by Ted Hughes

Children in role as the farmers at the end of the story of *The Iron Man*, use dramatic play to plant a garden in the village, so everyone will remember the events. They are also asked to create a plaque telling the story of the Iron Man for visitors to read.

An extra scene

Many stories contain opportunities for children to engage in whole group drama to create an extra chapter or scene without changing the existing narrative. This can involve taking on

Figure 10.1 A commemorative garden for The Iron Man

the role of an existing group within the story or inventing a new group who might interact with the story.

Use the following examples as models for other stories:

EXAMPLE 1: *THE OWL WHO WAS AFRAID OF THE DARK* BY JILL TOMLINSON

Children create an imaginary extra chapter at the end of this book. They play the role of some new human friends Plop made, after he cured his fear of the dark. They go for a night-time walk and meet the man with the telescope who wants to know what happened to Plop.

Planning and resources

- Children need to be familiar with the story before the activity.

You will need:

- A hall or cleared space for children to move around.
- A woolly scarf and a rolled paper to play the role of the man with the telescope.

Ages 7-11 (Years 2-6)

What to do

- Ask the children to help you make up and act out an extra chapter at the end of the story. Ask them to join you in pretending to be some new human friends Plop made, after he cured his fear of the dark. In this new chapter, the friends are going on a night time walk in the woods to see the good things about the dark for themselves.
- Talk about what they might see on the walk. Link with other books on nocturnal animals if appropriate such as **Night Animals: Usborne Beginners.**
- Ask the children to imagine that the space they are in is the woods and introduce the words '*action*' and '*freeze*' to start and stop the drama.
- On the word '*action*' start to prepare for the walk. Suggest the children do as you do in preparation. Using mimed actions, put on boots and a warm coat for the cooler night time temperatures and pack a torch and a special night time camera to photograph the creatures and the stars. Ask the children if they can think of anything else that might be useful to put in their backpacks and add those if appropriate.
- Keeping in role, ask the children to follow you in pairs as you walk to the centre of the woods with your torches. Walk around the room mentioning the dark trees and the stars as you go. Tell them you can see Orion and describe how you can identify it.
- Stop at a certain point, asking everyone to keep quiet, so as not to scare away the night time creatures. Children should then split up to quietly find nocturnal creatures to photograph. Plan to call everyone back with an owl sound.
- Call everyone together and ask if they managed to take some photographs.
- Pause the drama on the word '*freeze*' and use teacher narration to move the story on. Tell the children that you are now going to tell them what happened next in their extra chapter of the story. '*Just as the friends were about to return home, they met a man with a telescope who came to talk to them.*'
- Ask the children to pretend you are that man when you put on the scarf and hold the paper as a telescope. Remind the children what a telescope is before taking on the role.
- In role as the man, ask the children what they are doing in the woods. Mention that you are looking at the stars but you are scared of the night-time creatures. Ask the children what creatures they have seen and if they are dangerous. Tell them how you met a baby Owl recently who was too scared to fly in the dark and how you often wonder what happened to him. Wait for the children to provide the information about what has happened to Plop, before prompting them by asking if they have heard anything about the Owl. Keep in role as you ask questions about who helped Plop. Talk about how hard it is for people to face up to their fears and mention that talking to them about the night time creatures has helped you become less scared.
- Thank the children and narrate yourself out of role by taking off the scarf and saying *and the man with the telescope went away feeling much happier*.
- Resume your role as one of the friends and lead them back to the edge of the woods, talking about how much you are looking forward to seeing the photos. Make this a short walk and stop the drama with a narration saying: '*freeze. And the friends went home after a very interesting night time walk. And that is the end of our extra chapter.*'
- Ask the children which parts of the imaginary night time walk they enjoyed the most and praise them for helping the man with the telescope. Ask if they think they told him everything about Plop or did they miss anything out? Check the story if necessary.

- Ask a few children to describe the imaginary photos they took and suggest they draw them later.
- Praise the children for helping the man overcome his fear of the nocturnal woodland creatures.
- Talk about fears in general and link to other books on this issue if appropriate.

Reader reflections

Ask: 'Do you think readers would find our extra chapter interesting? Why do you think that?'

Extension activity

- Children draw and label their imaginary photos, with additional information about the creatures.
- Children write a diary entry about the woodland walk.
- Work with the children to write the events in the drama as the additional chapter.
- Read poems about the dark, such as **The Dark** and **The Shooting Stars** by James Carter from **Weird, Wild and Wonderful**.

EXAMPLE 2: *OLIVER AND THE SEAWIGS* BY PHILIP REEVE

In this activity, children create an extra scene in Chapter 3. They play the role of visitors to the island, helping Oliver find things to make Cliff a Seawig.

Planning and resources

You will need:

- A copy of the text to read aloud to the children.
- A large or cleared space.
- A scarf to play the role of Oliver.

What to do

- Read the text up to the part towards the end of Chapter 3, when Oliver says,

  Just think! What are the most wonderful things that an island could wear?

- Invite the children to make up an extra scene to this chapter by pretending to be some children and their teacher visiting the island, helping Oliver and Iris collect things for Cliff's Seawig.

- Ask the children to imagine that the room is Cliff the Island and that they are standing on the beach where Oliver stood shouting for his parents.
- Suggest that in this extra scene, the children help Oliver find interesting things on the beach and in the shallow part of the sea to make Cliff a good Seawig. They then place the items on top of Cliff to look like a wig.
- Talk as a group to discuss what suitable things they might find on the island, before asking the children to work in pairs or threes to decide what particular things they will look for when the drama starts. Make it clear that although they will need to mime the actions, they should talk as if it were really happening.
- Introduce the words *'action'* and *'freeze'* to start and stop the drama.
- Explain that in this extra part of the story, the teacher took a photo just before the children began their search. This will be represented in a freeze-frame, which comes alive to start the drama.
- Ask the children to decide how they will stand for the freeze. Provide some suggestions if necessary e.g. bending down to pick up some seaweed, wading out to sea, digging something up etc.
- Ask children to take up their frozen positions and then bring the freeze-frame to life on the word *'action.'*
- Let this run for a few minutes before stopping on the word *'freeze.'*
- Ask the children to sit beside the imaginary things they chose for the Seawig. Then agree a pathway for Oliver to walk round the children to see what they have found.
- When Oliver passes their found object, they should tell everyone what he sees or senses.
- Play the part of Oliver using the scarf as a sign of role. Walk slowly along the path, stopping at each object to hear the description. Briefly repeat the name of each object as you leave each one, to add status to the choices and ensure others keep engaged.
- Stop the drama on the word *'freeze'* and take off the scarf to come out of role.
- Read the rest of Chapter 3 to find out what Oliver and his friends found for the Seawig and compare it to the children's Seawig.

Reader reflections

After reading the whole story, ask the children: *'Would our extra scene make the story more interesting? Why do you think this?'*

Extension activities

- Children draw their contribution to the Seawig.
- Work with the children to create a written version of the extra scene e.g. *'As Oliver asked his question, some children and their teacher passed the island on a boat trip. They stopped at the island and Oliver asked them to help. This is what they found for Cliff's Seawig . . .'*

EXAMPLE 3: *THE NIGHT BUS HERO* BY ONJALI Q RAUF

Children play the role of teachers at a staff meeting in Hector's school, to discuss the problems he is causing and what they should do about it.

Planning and resources

- The children need to be familiar with the story up to the point in the chapter entitled *The Two Treasures*, when Mrs Vergara has phoned Hector's dad about his behaviour and the drawing.
- Decide on a name for yourself when you play the role of a different teacher. Choose a simple name that will not cause any distraction and be easy to remember.

You will need:

- A scarf or tie to indicate you will play the part of a member of the staff at Hector's school.

What to do

Preparation

- Ask the children to imagine they are the teachers at Hector's school, who have been called to a staff meeting to discuss his behaviour and what can be done about it.
- With reference to the text, discuss what the staff in Hector's school might know about him.
- Allow children a short time in pairs to decide what they will say about Hector as the teachers in the staff meeting and what they might suggest to help him improve his behaviour.
- Make a contract to use a scarf or tie to play the part of the teacher in charge of behaviour in the school and tell them what your new name will be.
- Use the words '*action*' and '*freeze*' to start and stop the drama.
- In role as the teacher i/c behaviour, thank the staff for coming to the meeting. Explain that Mrs Vergara has had to go home, as she is so upset. Explain how you are concerned about Hector and want to know what other staff have noticed regarding any problems in school. Wait for children in role as staff to respond.
- After collecting information, ask for suggestions on how to deal with Hector's problems. Discuss in role before stopping the drama.
- After reading the whole story discuss what impact an extra staffroom scene would have had on the story if it had been included. Talk about why the author may have chosen not to include a scene like this.

> **Extension activities**
>
> - Create a role-on-the-wall for Hector at this point in the story, with a view to looking at how he changes as the story progresses.
> - Children write up the staff meeting as an extra paragraph in the story.

Stepping into history

Stories and information texts linked to a historical period come alive when children engage in whole group drama based on the period. Whilst many historical venues and visiting actors provide excellent re-enactments, a whole group drama in school offers a differently challenging and emotionally engaging experience, with the potential to link more closely to a specific event or issue. If the drama is used as an introduction to a history topic, it can motivate children to read more about the historical setting and stories about the period.

The exact content of an imaginary experience will vary according to the historical period and/or the type of story, but they usually follow the three-part whole group drama sequence in some way.

EXAMPLE 1: FLORENCE NIGHTINGALE (YEARS 2-3)

Texts:

- *Vlad and the Florence Nightingale Adventure* by Kate and Sam Cunningham.
- *Herstory Book* by Katherine Halligan and Sarah Walsh.

Planning and resources

- Children need some basic background knowledge about the Crimean War and access to the text(s) for the reflection after the drama.

You will need:

- A large or cleared space.
- A shawl or scarf to play the role of a friend of Florence Nightingale.

What to do

The context

- Ask the children to pretend to be people who lived a long time ago at the time of the Crimean War. Explain that when the drama begins, you will need the children to be the nurses and their helpers who have sailed across the sea to help Florence Nightingale at the hospital in Scrutini. The nurses have come to look after the soldiers who were wounded in the Crimean war. Talk briefly about how different the nursing was in those days, without modern medicines and modern hospitals.

- Ask the children to pretend that the room they are in is the hospital. Describe the poor conditions they would see there. Agree what things in the room will not be used in the drama and stress that everything in the drama will need to be imagined.
- Ask the children to accept that you will play the part of a friend of Florence Nightingale when wearing the shawl or scarf as a sign of role. You have come to meet the nurses from the ship to tell them what to do.
- Use the words '*action*' and '*freeze*' to start and stop the drama.

The drama

- Start the drama on the word '*action*' and put on the shawl or scarf.
- In role as Florence's friend and fellow nurse, tell the nurses how grateful Florence Nightingale is for their help. Florence is currently busy in another part of the hospital but she sends some bad news: they will not be allowed to nurse the soldiers or look after them in any way due to the jealous doctor in charge. He will only let Florence and her nurses clean up the hospital wards. Stress the importance of the cleaning due to filthy conditions, such as food on the floor attracting rats and spreading disease.
- Explain that the doctor is always watching and checking up, so they need to do a good job with the cleaning. If they get Florence into trouble, they will all be sent home, leaving the soldiers with no one to look after them properly. Ask them to work quietly and carefully so they don't disturb the sick and wounded soldiers.
- Staying in role, use mimed actions to show the nurses how to open the imaginary cupboards, get the brooms and sweep the dirt into a bin using a shovel from the cupboard. Then ask the nurses to do the same.
- After a short while, ask the nurses to stop whilst you inspect what they have done so far. Stress the importance of cleanliness in the hospital and how Florence tries to keep everything clean. Walk around each area and ask who has swept each part. Give them praise for doing a good job.

Describe three more jobs that need doing:

1 *Washing the floor with mops*. Using mimed actions as before, demonstrate how to fill the buckets by the sinks and then get floor mops from the cupboard
2 *Wiping the tables next to the beds and round the windows*. Tell them where the cloths are kept and check they can remember where the sinks are.
3 *Fixing broken beds and windows*. Hammers and nails are in the cupboards but stress the need to work quietly so as not to disturb the soldiers.

- Then let the children choose which jobs they want to do.
- Keeping in role, offer praise and encouragement as the children work.

- Take off the sign of role and stop the drama.
- Move time on by narrating that the next time you say *action*, it will be two weeks later. Due to all the cleaning, the wards are looking better and some of the soldiers are smiling. But Florence Nightingale and her nurses are still cross because they are not allowed to nurse the soldiers. Then one day Florence sent an important message to all her nurses.
- Restart the drama on the word '*action*' and resume teacher-in-role. Tell the nurses that because more wounded soldiers are coming into the hospital, there are not enough people to look after them. So the doctor has said the nurses will be allowed to help look after the soldiers from tomorrow. They must be prepared. They need to cut up sheets for bandages, tidy the medicine cupboards and scrub the operating tables. Use mimed actions to indicate where these are in the room and let the children decide which jobs to do. Demonstrate these jobs if the children seem unsure.
- After a while, call the nurses to one side and ask what they have done. Tell them that Florence will be pleased. Tell the nurses about the term *Lady of the Lamp* and explain why Florence was called this by the soldiers. Then tell them that she has asked them to do the same. They should check the soldiers by walking among them with lamps. Suggest what they might do as they go around e.g. saying comforting words to the soldiers, tucking in blankets, giving medicines and water and fixing bandages. Tell the nurses to collect their lamps from the shelves around the room and start their rounds.
- Use the word '*freeze*' to stop the drama.
- Come out of role and narrate what happened next: '*The nurses did such a good job looking after the soldiers that several got better and some even went home. Then Queen Victoria sent a letter to Florence and her nurses saying how pleased she was with their work. After that, the doctor did not dare to stop Florence and the nurses from nursing the soldiers. Florence wanted to open a hospital in London when she got back home, so the nurses wrote to the newspapers telling them how good Florence was and how lots of soldiers got better because of the care she gave.*'

Reflection

Explain to the children that some things in the drama were similar to what really happened. Go over the main events and introduce the text(s). Invite the children to compare what the books tell us with the events they experienced in the drama.

EXAMPLE 2: STORIES ABOUT UK WORLD WAR 2 EVACUEES

Texts:

This activity can be linked to the many stories on the theme of U.K. Second World War evacuees, including the following:

- **Letters to the Lighthouse by Emma Carroll.**
- **The Valley of Lost Secrets by Lesley Parr.**

- ***Goodnight Mister Tom* by Michelle Magorian.**
- ***The Midnight Guardians* by Ross Montgomery.**

Planning and resources

- Children will need basic background knowledge about evacuees in the U.K. during the Second World War, including what the evacuees were allowed to take with them.

You will need:

- A list of games children played at that time.
- A hall or large space (it can be adapted to a smaller space).

What to do

The context

- Make a contract with the children to take on the roles of children from a city school, who are soon to be evacuated to an unknown area at the start of the Second World War.
- Ask the children to imagine the hall or classroom is part of a playground in their city school. It had been partly destroyed by a bomb the week before, so they have to play games that are suited to a small area such as skipping, marbles, throwing a small ball to each other, spinning tops etc. If you are not able to access a large space, talk about the kind of games they could play on a very small area of ground.
- Working in pairs, ask children to decide on a suitable game to play that they can mime for the drama. Then ask children to take up a frozen position in the imaginary playground, as if they were about to start their games.
- On the word '*action*' from you, the playground will come alive. Tell children to use mimed actions for the games but talk as if they were really there. They should do this until you stop the drama with the words '*freeze*' and '*relax*.' Let this activity run for a few minutes.
- (Optional) Ask half the class to demonstrate their games to the other half, who try to guess what they are. Then swap over so the other half demonstrates.
- Move time on to the day before the evacuation. Ask the children to decide on one small item they will take with them in their evacuee bag, to remind them of home. Talk about what they were allowed and not allowed to take e.g. they were not allowed to take their pets. Suggest a few possibilities such as a photo of a family member or their pet, a favourite book or toy or an item passed down to them by the family etc.
- On the word '*action*,' every child should find a space on their own in the hall or classroom. Explain that this space will represent their bedroom on the day they left home as an evacuee.
- Demonstrate how you would like them to mime lifting a small bag down from the top of a tall cupboard or wardrobe and pack it with a few things, including the item that will remind them of home. Stress that they are to do this in silence as they are alone in their rooms. However, when they have packed their bags, they should make their way to the station, where they meet and talk to the other evacuees.

- Designate an area of the room to represent the station.
- Suggest that when they get to the station they might talk to each other about what they have packed and what they are feeling as they wait for the train. When they have finished talking they should just stand and wait for the train. Warn them that you will stop the drama at some point during the talking, by saying the word *'freeze.'*

The drama

- Let the drama activity continue for a few minutes to allow all children to pack their bags and talk to someone else at the imaginary station.
- Freeze the action and then walk amongst the children, inviting individuals to speak out their thoughts as evacuees when you point to them or touch them on the shoulder.
- Stop the drama.
- Out of role, ask the children to share what their special item was.

Pose a problem

- Ask the children to plan a whole class freeze-fame of the moment the villagers saw the evacuees arrive. Ask the class what kind of villagers would be there e.g. children, hosts, a teacher, a shopkeeper, a farmer. Talk about what the villagers might be looking forward to and what they might be concerned about.
- Talk about what the evacuees might be looking forward to and what they might be worried about when they saw the villagers.
- Divide the class into two groups for the freeze-frame: the evacuees and the villagers. Ask the children to decide what their group might be thinking at that moment.
- Make the freeze-frame and use thought tracking or a Thought Bubble to invite children to speak out what their character might be thinking.
- Discuss how these worries might be overcome for both sides and then working in groups ask the children to make freeze-frames showing an action that could help bring the groups together e.g. a welcome party by the hosts, showing the evacuees around the village or evacuees helping the hosts with some jobs.

Reflect

- Link and compare the drama experience with the events in your chosen text(s).
- Talk about similar situations that can occur nowadays.

> **Reader reflections**
>
> Ask:
>
> - *'Do readers need to know a lot about the historical period to enjoy a story set in the past?'*

- 'What other stories have you/we read that are set in the past? Do you have any favourites and if so why do you like these?'
- 'How important is it for stories set in the past to include accurate historical details?'

EXAMPLE 3: THE CHILDREN'S MUSEUM

This approach is based on the mantle-of-the-expert drama strategy. It places children in an imaginary situation where they are asked to provide ideas for a themed room in a children's museum. It creates an imaginary purpose for reading information texts about specific historical periods, events, authors or famous people and works well as a background to historically based stories. It can also be adapted to become a room based on a particular story or series. The challenge to select and present the information accurately in an interesting and accessible way for a children's museum, requires careful reading for meaning.

The room in the children's museum can be presented as a fun place to visit or a more serious place, depending on the subject matter. If the subject matter touches on sensitive historical issues or events, you will need to discuss how best to communicate sensitive information in an appropriate way. It may also be useful to share how real museums tackle this.

The information gained during the activity can provide audience and purpose for writing biographies of famous people or summaries of historical events for the museum's book shop or website.

Other versions include ideas for themed rooms in environmental centres, space centres, science centres, art galleries etc., each requiring children to read information texts relevant to the venue.

Texts:

The Museum drama can link to the reading of a wide range of historically based texts, including the following:

- **The Wild Way Home by Sophie Kirtley:** The Stone Age
- **Secrets of a Sun King by Emma Carroll:** The Ancient Egyptians
- **The Curse of the Maya by Johnny Pearce and Andy Loneragan:** The Maya
- **The Queen's Fool by Ally Sherrick:** The Tudors
- **Black Powder by Ally Sherrick:** The Gunpowder Plot
- **The Last Post by Keith Campion:** World War One
- **Arctic Star by Tom Palmer:** The World War Two Arctic convoy to Russia
- **Counting on Katherine by Helaine Becker:** Space travel
- **Hidden Figures by Margot Lee Shetterly**
- **Voices Series:** Scholastic
- **True Adventures Series:** Pushkin Press

Planning and resources

- Children need access to information texts relevant to your chosen topic, character, story or theme.
- Compose a letter from a museum director requesting ideas for a themed room in a local children's museum. The letter should give the following information:

You are a new director of a local museum. You have been given some money to convert a large empty space into a room for children based on the theme of (name the historical period, character or event in your chosen text). You are not sure what will appeal to children so you are asking local children for their ideas. All ideas should be accompanied by information sheets about the room suitable for children to read.

You will need:

- Images and other information about museums as required.
- Relevant information texts for each small group of children.

What to do

- Ask the children to take part in a drama where their school has been contacted by the director of a new museum for children that will be opening nearby.
- Use the images and information to ensure children understand the concept of a museum and a director.
- Invite children to share their experiences of museums and ask them what kinds of things work well for children in museums. If the museum focuses on a sensitive historical issue, then talk about how the information can be communicated in a respectful way.
- Read out the letter from the museum director. Make sure children understand that this is an imaginary situation and ask them to imagine they accepted this challenge.
- Arrange the children into small groups and provide them with access to relevant information texts to support their information sheets and ideas.
- Ask the class to imagine they are to be interviewed for a local radio station about their ideas for the museum. Talk about what questions they might be asked and what they would want to say.
- Then either ask groups to improvise the interview with one child being the radio host, or play the radio host yourself and interview them as a whole class.
- Finish with a class freeze-frame depicting a photo of the children in the media, along with a suitable headline.

Link to a text

- Make links between your chosen text(s) and the knowledge children gained about the historical period during the drama experience.

> **Reader reflections**
>
> Ask: *'Do you prefer reading about history through stories or information books? Why do you think this?'*

Extension activities

- Children sketch or draw a plan of their contribution to the themed room in the museum.
- Children make pop-up boxes with information about their theme for a display in the museum.

Further suggestions

- **AN ART GALLERY:** Replace the museum with an art gallery. Children read information texts about different artists. Link to ***The Boy who Fooled the World*** **by Lisa Thompson.**
- **A WILD LIFE CENTRE**: Replace the museum with a local Wildlife Centre. Children read information texts about woodland plants and creatures. Link to ***By Ash, Oak and Thorn*** **by Melissa Harrison.**

Offering advice

This activity illustrates how the mantle-of-the-expert strategy works within the context of a whole group drama to deepen children's understanding of a text by asking them to take on knowledgeable roles in order to advise the characters in a story. This approach can also be used to create an imaginary audience and purpose for reading information books in order to advise an invented character linked to a story or historical event.

Planning

- Choose part of a story or historical event, where someone might need help or advice to solve a problem e.g. how Londoners could build a safer city after the Great Fire of London.
- Select an appropriate collective role for the children where they can give advice or help a character e.g. fire officers in London after the Great Fire. Alternatively you can invent new roles where children become professional experts such as researchers, investigators, journalists or curators who can provide advice relating to the events in the story e.g. historical experts advise on creating a living museum for the Great Fire of London.
- If children are playing professional roles, the drama can be paused to enable them to read information texts in order to gain sufficient background knowledge for the drama.

Resources

- If the roles are sedentary such as researchers or investigators, the drama can take place in the classroom, but if the drama involves meeting characters in their own worlds, then a larger space may be more appropriate.
- You may need a few basic props/resources such as a scarf to indicate you are playing teacher-in-role or a letter from a character asking for help.

What to do

Proceed as in the overview of this chapter, with the following adaptations:

- Use a letter or teacher-in-role to pose a problem that requires the children to give advice or help.
- Stop the drama if children need more information in order to help, and restart when they are ready to pass on what they know. This could mean stopping the drama for some time before resuming.
- When children have solved the problems and/or helped the characters, stop the drama to reflect on the impact of their expertise and discuss any universal links with those who help others.
- Read the text and talk about how the drama experience links to it.

Extension activities

- Children talk and/or record how they helped the character.
- Send a thank you letter to the children as if from the character.

EXAMPLE: *THE HODGEHEG* BY DICK KING-SMITH

Planning, resources and what to do

- This example is designed as an introduction to the book for Years 2/3.
- You will need a scarf or similar item to play the role of Max's friend.
- Ask the children where people can cross roads in safety and what to do if there are no designated places to cross. Talk about how difficult it is for wild animals to cross busy roads.
- Read children the story up to the end of Chapter 1, where Max sets out to solve the problem of how the hedgehogs can safely cross the road to the park.
- Ask the children to pretend to be road safety officers who have been asked to help Max with his research by a friend of his.
- Let children share ideas in pairs before coming together as a class to talk about ways to help hedgehogs cross the road in safety. Investigate the potential of all ideas.
- Use the words '*action*' and '*freeze*' to start and stop the drama.

- Use the scarf to take on the role of Max's friend.
- In this role talk about how your friend Max the hedgehog has gone off to see if he can find a way for hedgehogs to cross the road in safety. You want to help Max so you are hoping the road safety officers will have some ideas.
- Challenge the children to offer clear explanations and descriptions of their ideas and the likely success of each one before thanking them for their help.
- Take off your scarf and narrate your way out of the drama with the words: *'freeze. So Max's friend went away feeling very pleased with the ideas from the safety officers. Would Max succeed or would he need the safety officers' ideas?'*
- Read the rest of the book to discover whether Max found a way for the hedgehogs to cross safely.
- Compare Max's solution to those offered by the safety officers.

A similar story

This activity involves using whole group drama to create a version of a story, topic or theme, where children are confronted with similar problems to those in the texts. When children have a similar experience to related texts, they go on to read those texts from a more informed perspective, creating greater curiosity and a desire to make comparisons between their own experience and those expressed in the texts. This experience also helps give children the confidence to make comparisons between similar aspects in other stories.

Planning, resources and what to do

- This activity needs careful planning to ensure the children have a similar but different experience to the one in the chosen story. The drama may last for one lesson or a series of lessons. It may focus on the whole story, part of a story, or one aspect of a topic or theme. Whatever the duration, it needs to be emotionally engaging to provide an effective introduction to the text. The emotional pull of whole group drama means it can sustain pauses to accommodate other drama strategies to challenge children's thinking. It can also accommodate time spent back in the classroom on background reading and/or written work between drama lessons without losing momentum.
- The content of the drama should either follow part of the plotline of your chosen story or relate to a similar theme.
- The exact content of the drama will vary according to the events in your story, but the following examples can be used as a guide:

EXAMPLE 1: *AN ALIEN IN THE JAM FACTORY* BY CHRISSIE SAINS

In this activity, children move from making machine movements and sounds to operating the machines in role as workers in *The Juicy Sweet Factory*. This creates an experience of a factory context, similar to the jam factory in the text.

188   *Ages 7-11 (Years 2-6)*

Planning and resources

- Children need access to the book after the activity but keep it hidden prior to and during the drama.

You will need:

- A few images of machines in a food factory.
- A whistle or a harsh sounding metallic instrument such as a cowbell
- A clipboard and/or an overall or tabard to play the role of the factory supervisor.
- A sign saying **The Juicy Sweet Factory**.
- A large or cleared space

What to do

- Show the children the Juicy Sweet Factory sign and ask them what kinds of sweets would be made in a factory with this name. Talk about the types of machines the factory workers might use and what movements and sounds these machines might make, such as moving repetitively up and down or round and round.
- Ask the children to stand in a large rectangular shape to represent the walls of the Juicy Sweet Factory and invite them to pretend to be the factory machine operators.
- Allow pairs time to invent and practise a simple sequence of movements for operating their machine along with appropriate sounds.
- Number the machines and explain that when you say the word '*action*' you will pull an imaginary lever, to start the machines. They will start one at a time. Pair number 1 will be the first to start their machine sounds and movements, followed by the other pairs in numerical order until all the machines are working.
- Start the drama and pause it after the last pair have performed their movements.
- Repeat the activity, so children gain confidence with the process.
- Explain how you are now going to bring The Juicy Sweet Factory to life on an ordinary working day. The machines will come to life as before but without the sounds, so the workers operating their machines can talk to each other as they operate their machines.
- Ask the children to pretend you are the supervisor when you wear the overall and/or carry the clip board etc. You will be visiting each machine to check things are going well. If their machine breaks down, the children should imagine there are tools in the centre of the room to fix it.
- Bring the factory to life, using the supervisor role to develop children's vocabulary and skills in explaining how well their machines are working etc.

The Problem

- Pause the drama and come out of role. Narrate that the supervisor stopped the machines to call everyone to an emergency meeting in the centre of the factory. On the word '*action*' resume your role as supervisor and ask the operators to sit around you.

Tell the workers you have had to stop the machines because the new owner has let his pet hamster into the factory and it has left droppings and hairs in the sweet flavourings. All the machines will now have to be cleaned as they could be contaminated with germs from the hamster. Talk about how bad this is. If word gets out in the media then the factory could be closed down and everyone would lose their jobs. Ask the workers to use the sinks and the cleaning materials in the middle of the factory to clean their machines.

- Stop the cleaning after a short while and call the workers back to the centre. Tell them that the new owner wants them to think of new flavours for all the sweets so he can sell more packets. Talk about how you saw the owner using binoculars to spy on another sweet factory across the road. Ask the workers what they think the owner might be up to.
- Stop the drama.

Link to the text

- Show children the cover of **The Alien in the Jam Factory** and ask them to speculate on how it might link with their drama.
- Read the story to the children, stopping now and again to ask if they notice any similarities and/or differences between their drama and the plot of this story.

Extension activities

Children can:

- Draw and label their machines and write instructions on how to operate them.
- Write a page in a new inventions book for making sweets, similar to the one written by Scooter in the story.

EXAMPLE 2: *THE SHARK CALLER* BY ZILLAH BETHELL

This activity involves a preparatory classroom lesson followed by a whole group drama session in a larger space. This example focuses on the issue of conservation versus tourism as an introduction to one of the themes in **The Shark Caller,** but it could be linked to other books with a similar theme.

Planning and resources

- This activity is designed as an introduction to *Wanpela:* the first chapter of the text.
- The preparatory work takes place in the classroom.

You will need:

- A hall or cleared space for the drama work.
- A scarf as a sign of teacher-in-role.
- Information texts about sharks.
- (Optional) Other texts on similar themes.

What to do

In the classroom

- Make a contract with the children, asking them to play the role of the inhabitants of a small imaginary island in the Pacific Ocean called Shark Island. The islanders survive by fishing and growing their own food. They have lived on this island for many generations with little access to technology. The island is beautiful but under-developed and remote. It also has sharks around the island which they used to hunt and kill for food. Now there are fewer sharks and the islanders have other food, so they no longer hunt them. They make trinkets for tourists which they exchange for goods via a supply boat from the mainland.
- Draw out a simple map of the island, asking the children to add a few features but keep it very sparse and under-developed.
- Allow the children to access information books on sharks in preparation for the drama. The amount of time you spend on this will depend on your circumstances and the needs of the children. It may be a written activity where children record 3 to 5 interesting facts about sharks or a whole class activity where you read extracts from some of the books to the class.
- Explain that the drama will start with an annual ceremony called The Day of the Boats, which the island ancestors believed would protect them from the sharks in the days when they hunted them. Each family cleans and decorates their boat before gathering by the shore to hold a short ceremony.
- Help the children plan a simple ceremony ready for the drama and ask the children to pretend you will be an island Elder helping to organise it. As this role is one of the group, you don't need to use an item of clothing to represent the role, unless you find it helpful.
- Organise the children into small groups representing boat owning adults living on the island and ask them to plan how they will decorate their boats and prepare for the ceremony when the drama starts.

In a large space

Introduction

- Ask the children to imagine that the room they are in represents the part of the island where the Day of the Boats Ceremony will take place. If necessary define any areas or items in the room that will not be part of the drama.
- Introduce/remind them of the words *'action'* and *'freeze'* to start and stop the drama at any point.

- Make it clear that although they need to talk as if it were really happening, all the actions need to be mimed. Provide some suggestions if necessary e.g. washing the boats with imaginary buckets of water and cloths.
- Allow groups time to decide what job/ activity they will be miming when the drama begins and a frozen position for starting their first action.

Building belief/ dramatic play

- Start with a whole class freeze-frame of preparations for The Day of the Boats. Children should take up a frozen position as if they were just about to start their first job of the day. Bring the preparations to life on the word '*action*.' In role as the Elder, move around the groups to offer help and ask questions.
- Pause the drama to organise the enactment of the ceremony based on the children's ideas and then resume the drama to perform it.
- Stop the drama on the word '*freeze*.'

The problem

- Out of role, tell the children that time moved on to the day after the ceremony, when the Elder called an important meeting.
- Restart the drama and in role as the Elder, pass on the following information. You have received a letter from a wealthy businesswoman who lives on the mainland. She wants the islanders to recreate their ancient shark hunting trips for tourists. She will pay them large sums of money. She makes the point that they won't have to kill the sharks every time, just now and again to keep the tourists interested. She says it will attract more tourists to the island, so the islanders can have a better standard of living. She will be sending a representative to explain more details and answer any questions.
- Allow the islanders some time to respond at the meeting. Bring out the benefits and drawbacks of tourists on the island.
- Pause the drama.
- Ask the children to accept that you will play the part of the businesswoman's representative when wearing the scarf. Ask them what questions they would like to ask this person.
- Restart the drama.
- In role as the representative stress the advantages of the businesswoman's proposal e.g. sharks are dangerous, so killing a couple will be a good thing; it will bring greater prosperity to the island so they can all enjoy a better life; Islanders can charge tourists to watch the Blessing of the Boats ceremony and it will bring the ancient ceremonies back to life. Try to present the arguments in a reasonable and genuine manner so children are willing to listen. Leave the meeting telling the Islanders they must think carefully before replying as they may not get this opportunity again.
- Stop the drama with the words '*freeze . . . and the representative went away,*' and then take off the scarf.

- Resume the role of the Elder and ask the Islanders for their responses to the representative's arguments.
- Suggest that each person talks with their friends about what they should do and meet up later to decide how to reply.
- Pause the drama to organise a spotlighting activity.
- Ask children to sit in their groups as if they were about to discuss the businesswoman's proposal.
- Allow children a few minutes in silence to plan what they will say when the conversation in their group is brought to life. Remind them that everyone in their group must be given a chance to express their opinion. This is a spontaneous improvisation with all groups talking at the same time with no audience.
- Start the improvisations on the word '*action*' but freeze them after a short while.
- Explain the spotlighting strategy where you will walk around the groups in turn, bringing them to life for a short time so everyone can hear snippets of their conversation.
- Remind those groups not in the spotlight to remain silent so everyone can hear. If some groups have quiet voices it may be helpful to summarise what they have said before moving on to spotlight the next group.
- Re-start the drama after the spotlighting. Call the children together for another meeting to discuss their current thoughts about the businesswoman's proposal. Take a vote to decide a reply and stop the drama.
- Discuss if similar situations happen in real life and if so when, where and what have been the outcomes.

Link to the text

- Read the first chapter of **The Shark Caller** entitled *Wanpela* and ask the children to make links with this chapter and the events in their drama.

Reader reflections

- After or during the reading of the rest of **The Shark Caller**, invite the children to identify other themes in the book e.g. time, friendship and coping with loss. Ask which theme had the most impact on them as readers and why.
- Ask if the children if they have read any other books with similar themes to those in this book and discuss those. Alternatively select books yourself and invite the children to identify any which touch on similar themes e.g. **The Last Bear** by Hannah Gold.

Further suggestions

- **The Iron Man by Ted Hughes:** Children engage in dramatic play as villagers and farmers living near a river. They hear news that an Iron Woman has come out of the river and is eating all the cars and iron railings. What should they do?

- **Theseus and the Minotaur:** Children engage in dramatic play, as young people loading a sailing ship to go on a voyage with the Prince, as commanded by the King. As they set sail, the Prince explains how they are to be sacrificed to a beast in a labyrinth, but he has plans to kill it first. Can they advise him how to kill it? How do they feel and do they believe he will succeed?
- **Land of Roar by Jenny McLachlan:** Children create their own imaginary land of adventures and magical creatures to play in. They engage in dramatic play to pack bags to take with them on their first visit. What adventures might they have and what useful things do they need to take? They are led through a portal to visit the place, making camp before they set off. They tell each other what area they plan to visit first. The drama is paused to allow each group to create and share a freeze-frame depicting what happened to them during their most exciting adventure in this land. Read the description on the back of the book. Will the Land of Roar be anything like their land?

Conclusion

I can think of no better way to conclude this book than by sharing the words of some of the children and teachers who have inspired me to carry on talking and writing about the potential of drama to support learning. I began to use drama-in-education thirteen years after I qualified as a teacher and I can still recall some of the challenges it presented. However, I can also recall the time when a silent, withdrawn 10-year-old boy began to join in with the actions during a whole group drama, whispering a few words to a fellow classmate about what he was doing. I can still recall the look on the face of a neglected 8-year-old boy with special needs, as he successfully led his class through the tangles of an imaginary forest, and I can still feel the commitment of a Year 6 class who refused to go out to play because they wanted to finish the drama. I can also hear the voice of the 5-year-old who told me how much she enjoyed the drama because her mummy had sandals just like mine. But that's another story!

I write this book in the hope that one day, the potential for drama to support reading for meaning will be acknowledged by every educational institution and access to drama-in-education will be an entitlement for every teacher.

What the children said

YEAR 1: Snow White
'The huntsman left Snow White in the woods. He was feeling sad. He didn't want to do it.'

YEAR 2/3: Information texts about gravity
'What I have learnt is that Isaac Newton was clever and always thinking about how things worked and when we were outside playing, I wished we still went there.'

YEAR 4: Theseus and the Minotaur
'I liked . . . when Prince Theseus killed the Minotaur. When he chopped the Minotaur's head off. I did not like the bit where Prince Theseus' father jumped off the cliff.'

YEAR 5/6: *The Highwayman* by A. Noyes
'I was able to know how Tim felt. I then knew how much guilt Tim had.'

What the teachers said

During 2018-19 I supported 12 primary school teachers from Waterton Multi-Academy Trust to conduct some action research on the impact of drama on literacy. It was a privilege to work with such enthusiastic and dedicated teachers. Here are just a few of their observations:

EYFS: *Rama and Sita*
'We read the story of Rama and Sita ... and created freeze-frames for key story events. The children sequenced the story to create a zig zag book.'

Year 1: Goldilocks
'When we completed the Goldilocks and the three bears drama activity, it had a big impact on language ... having three focuses (thoughts, feelings and what each character would have said) helped the children give specific and targeted responses. . .. We had the chance to discuss different synonyms for the word "mad." A year 1 child then gave an example of "furious." As a group we then got the chance to discuss this word and why this is a better word to use than mad.'

Year 2
'It gave them a sense of ownership which meant they were highly engaged throughout.'
'Children were able to give evidence for their ideas about characters' thoughts and feelings much more confidently.'

Year 3
'The children really enjoyed the drama and with that came an enthusiasm that set us up for the week ahead. They were allowed to really think about each character in the story at a specific time. This helped to unpick emotions and thoughts as well as general observances. Because the children had the opportunity to put themselves in the character's shoes, they could have conversations and speak as if they were them. This supported their understanding of the specific point at which we had stopped, also it helped to practise vocabulary verbally ... it had such a distinct impact.'

Year 4: *The Firework Maker's Daughter* by P. Pullman
'We did the "journey drama" round the corridors and took a trip through the jungle as Lila (out of *The Firework Maker's Daughter*). We saw all of the leaves/flowers and experienced everything that she did.'
'The drama helped to teach empathy, which is such a difficult concept to know how to develop with children.'

Year 5/6: Class novels
'The drama ... allowed the children to understand concepts to a greater depth ... perspectives that were difficult for children to grasp are now easier to explain.'
'Children were able to comprehend more complex parts of class novels and write about them, answering questions about various chapters or parts of chapters.'

Wild horses and magic

I leave you with a piece of writing from Katherine in Year 3 and a comment from a Year 4 teacher that I will always remember. The writing followed a whole group drama activity linked to information texts and stories about the natural world and protecting the environment. The children worked with me to create a beautiful place; a natural environment for visitors to enjoy. However, as responsible owners they were faced with the competing demands of conservation versus the needs of the economy. This is what Katherine wrote:

My favourite bit was when I was catching a wild horse. But the factory could be built if there was a pipe coming out of the wall and going somewhere else.

I had an idea what their solutions to the factory problem might be, but I had no idea there was a wild horse in this beautiful place until I read this. Such is the power of drama to unlock a child's imagination. If we can apply this powerful teaching method to claw texts off the page and make them live, we can put those texts under the microscope to examine them more closely and hold them up to the light to explore the layers of meaning.

As a Year 4 teacher once said to me, after his challenging class explored a text in drama with uncharacteristic enthusiasm: *'Drama must be some kind of magic.'*

The drama strategies

The following drama strategies are arranged in alphabetical order and have been selected on the basis of their potential to develop reading for meaning. They include most of the well-known, tried and tested approaches to drama, but do not represent a comprehensive list. Suggestions on how to make the best use of the strategies have been added to the definitions where appropriate.

Drama is made up of a number of different strategies to be selected according to the learning objectives and the needs of the children. Whilst many of the strategies are useful as one-off classroom activities, they are most effective when incorporated into a sustained whole group drama experience.

Action/freeze narration

Best suited to children in Years R to 4, Action/Freeze Narration allows all the children to physically re-enact a sequence of events according to the teacher's narration. Children mime the actions individually but alongside each other, all playing the same character following the same narration. The events are presented in sequential sections with the children miming the actions on the word '*action*' and stopping on the word '*freeze*' each time. Whilst this activity requires careful listening during the narration, it involves discussion between each section on what happens next and how best to portray the characters and events.

Actions

An abstract way of portraying real-life everyday activities and events, actions can be mimed or accompanied by sounds or speech. They can also be a way of expressing abstract concepts such as scientific processes or geographical features as part of an embodied approach to learning. Their function in the context of drama-in-education is to build belief in an imaginary context or encourage thoughtful consideration and expression of meaning rather than producing an accurate theatrical performance.

Character circle

Originally employed by actors to explore relationships between one of the main characters and the other characters in a play, the Character Circle can be adapted to enable children to examine relationships in stories or plays where there are several characters. Each child or group is assigned to a different character in the story, other than the main character. Children are given time to decide how their character feels about the main character based on what they know of the text. The children sit in a circle around an empty chair representing the main character to share their views. Another version is to ask a confident child to sit in the chair as the main character, to respond to what the other characters say.

Communal voice

Two groups represent the individual voices of two different characters in conversation. The two groups stand opposite each other. When one of the group speaks, they take on the role of their assigned character, using the words *I* and *me* whenever they speak. Different children in the group take turns to represent the voice of their character, but each contributor must pick up and continue the thread of the conversation. Communal Voice helps children explore characters' motives, feelings and relationships at significant moments in a story, but it can also link to topics and information texts. For example a modern character can talk to a historical character or to someone living in another geographical area and creatures can hold imaginary conversations about habitats or climate change.

Conscience alley/decision alley/conscience forest

In Conscience Alley, the class is divided into two groups to represent two conflicting, polarized sides of an argument or point of view. When used to develop reading for meaning, the arguments are usually based on a fictional character facing a dilemma or issues in a non-fiction text. Children are often asked to represent arguments from the text which may not align with their own views. Where this is the case, they should be given an opportunity to express their own views after the activity. In the traditional Conscience Alley, the two opposing sides face each other in two lines to form an alleyway or corridor. A child or teacher-in-role as a character, walks slowly between the two lines as if walking down the alley. Children speak to the character as they walk down the alley, presenting pre-prepared reasoned arguments to try to persuade them of their given point of view. The character can walk down one side of the alleyway to hear one side of the argument, then back along the opposite side to hear the other side or walk down the centre listening to alternate views.

Conscience Alley can be adapted to become an imaginary public debate or trial in which some children take on roles to present two polarised points of view, whilst others vote or play the part of a jury.

Another version of Conscience Alley is Conscience Forest where a character's confused thoughts are revealed in a dream. In this version the children stand like trees in a tangled forest rather than an alley. The character walks among the children, who whisper the character's inner thoughts. This version can be used in a classroom with children sitting at desks.

Dreamscapes

Children use key words and phrases from the text to create a dream sequence. It's often used to demonstrate how words can evoke menacing moods in poems, novels and plays. There are many ways to produce a dream sequence, ranging from an audio recording of key words and phrases to a physical interpretation such as a version of Conscience Forest. There is also an option to combine the words with music and dance.

Echo

The Echo is designed to improve an actor's performance delivering lines or reciting a text. It focuses mainly on developing the skills of clarity, audibility and confidence when performing to an audience. The reader reads one of their lines to the rest of the group, who then echo it so the performer has a sense of how an audience might hear and receive it. It works best if the teacher models the process, making deliberate mistakes for the children to identify e.g. reading too quietly, with head down, timidly etc.

Forum theatre

The whole class/group (the forum) work with the teacher to direct a small group improvisation as it takes place. It can be adapted to enable a class of children to direct and produce an authentic freeze-frame based on a text.

Freeze

Children take up a frozen position, usually in character. The effect is similar to a pause in a video clip. Freezing characters can slow down the action to facilitate discussion and reflection on the text, as well as providing a means to pause or stop the drama.

Freeze-frames (tableaux or still image)

A small group of children physically depict a significant moment from a text by freezing the action, as if in a frame. The freeze-frames are usually shown to the rest of the class. When combined with forum theatre, freeze-frames are an effective way to enable observation, investigation and analysis of a text by the whole class. They support reading for meaning by developing the skills of inference and deduction and encouraging empathy. Illustrations and photos in books can also be used as a stimulus for a freeze-frame and children can create freeze-frames to represent their own ideas for illustrations. Freeze-frames have a wide range of uses including making a sequenced storyboard with multiple freeze-frames and captions, expressing predictions and forming a basis for improvised dialogue when brought to life. This can also be a valuable way for groups to represent the main ideas in information texts, such as the digestive system, gravity and the solar system, where they use their bodies in a more abstract way to provide evidence of their understanding.

Guided tour

One child leads a partner on an imaginary guided tour around the setting of a story. It can be based an illustration, a map or a written description. Roles are then reversed to travel back. Alternatively the teacher leads all the children on an imaginary guided tour to describe the setting. This activity works best as a physical tour with the children walking around the room. If space is limited children can sit with their eyes closed as the teacher describes the setting as if they were walking through it.

Hot-seating

A person or a group take on a role when sitting on a designated chair or seat, in order to answer questions. Hot-seating can be a powerful tool in helping children to empathise with characters or gain a deeper understanding of the consequences of events in a text. It can also bring children closer to the text by offering different perspectives, bringing the events alive through the eyes of the characters. It can be applied to non-fiction texts allowing children to ask questions of animals, birds, sea life and insects.

Consider the most appropriate character for the hot-seat in relation to your objectives. The protagonist in a story may not be the best one to challenge the thinking of the group. In some stories a main character may prove so unpopular that it would be difficult for the children to respond without prejudice or they may react in an extreme manner. In some cases it may be better to hot-seat a minor or invented character who could answer questions about the main character, such as a neighbour, relative or friend. There are versions of hot-seating involving groups rather than individuals, but whatever form it takes, hot-seating relies on the knowledge and understanding of those in the hot-seat, so preparation is required if children are to take on this role instead of the teacher.

Hot-seating can provide opportunities for children to develop their questioning skills but they often need support to devise appropriately focused questions. This provides an opportunity for children to consider questions in relation to audience and purpose.

Improvisations

There are two different types of improvisation: Spontaneous and Polished:

In Spontaneous Improvisation, children talk in role without preparation, often in pairs or small groups. The improvisations can be performed by one group in front of an audience or several groups can improvise simultaneously without an audience. Sometimes the groups stop to listen to snippets of each other's improvisations (see Spotlighting).

Polished Improvisations are planned and rehearsed before they are shared.

Both kinds of improvisations can be reworked and rehearsed to form the basis of a scripted performance.

Whilst improvisations allow children the freedom to express themselves in role, the content should always be in line with school values.

Letters from characters

Children are sent imaginary letters from characters asking them for help, advice or information. They can also provide new information to move the drama on.

Line-up

Children representing characters are lined up by the class on a continuum from the highest to the lowest, according to a given criteria. Discussion arises from the need for whole class agreement or as a response to a line-up made by an individual child or the teacher. Characters can be lined up according to criteria such as their status within the setting, from the kindest to the cruellest, the most influential to the least influential and even the most popular to the least popular with the class etc. Placing the more minor characters on the continuum in relation to each other can provoke valuable in-depth discussion.

Mantle-of-the-expert

The term 'mantle-of-the-expert' was used by the drama-in-education pioneer Dorothy Heathcote in the 1970s, to describe the technique where children take on the role and responsibilities of experts, commissioned by someone to undertake an important task. The roles are often those of professionals such as architects, historians, museum curators and designers and can involve researching information from non-fiction texts.

Children move in and out of the drama to perform the tasks, seek more information and reflect or solve problems. The teacher usually works in role alongside the children with equal power and authority during the drama. The term comes from the idea of throwing expertise onto the shoulders of the children like a mantle or a cloak. It is used in many schools as a key approach to teaching and learning alongside other strategies.

In this book the Mantle-Of-The-Expert strategy has been adapted and extended to include any roles where children are in a position to give others help and advice.

Object game

Children imagine they are objects in a setting, describing what they might see, feel and sense without naming the object. Others try to guess which object they are describing, then discuss how the object came to be there and why they think the author included it. Objects can include other non-human things such as animals, insects, birds, plants, buildings etc.

Pathway

This is similar to Conscience Alley where children arrange themselves to form a pathway for a character or a visitor to travel through. However, in the pathway strategy, the children describe what the traveller might see or sense as they walk along. Children can organise themselves to create a winding path or use their bodies to form features for the traveller to negotiate e.g. pairs join hands to form an arch for the traveller to walk under or groups make an obstacle for them to step over or around. This strategy is a useful way to examine and recreate aspects of a setting in a text and is sometimes used in conjunction with the guided tour strategy.

Playscripts

A playscript is a written text designed to become a theatrical performance. Theatre is organic and involves a team effort with all the separate elements working together to tell a story. Playscripts written for whole school productions provide large numbers of children with a valuable and memorable theatrical experience, whereas shorter classroom playscripts or single scenes from longer plays, provide more opportunity to focus on reading for meaning via the medium of a script. The need to read and perform lines with appropriate expression, either individually or chorally, provides children with an opportunity to extend their vocabulary by considering the meaning and significance of key words and phrases in a shared text. Short playscripts designed for single classes of children include historical, environmental and scientific topics, adaptations of novels and melodramatic versions of Shakespeare and classic stories. Some plays are based on characters from reading schemes and include versions of traditional stories.

Puppet-in-role

Younger children find puppets engaging and are only too willing to help them solve problems within a story. Puppet-in-role works best with a glove puppet or one that can be manipulated to indicate emotions. They can be a useful introduction to stories with animal or fantasy characters, but the puppet does not have to be the main character. You can invent a role for the puppet such as a concerned friend of the main character or someone who might have witnessed the problems and wants to solve them. The puppet usually communicates by whispering to the teacher, who relays what has been said to the children, thus avoiding the need to be a ventriloquist. Finding the puppet in a sad or confused state increases the children's level of engagement but it's important to maintain the puppet's responses throughout the activity, because in the child's mind making the puppet feel better is the main objective.

Puppets on sticks

Stick puppets representing specific characters provide younger children with an opportunity to wave their puppets whenever their character speaks during a story reading. They can also join in with any repeated words or refrains spoken by their character. They also help children identify passages of direct speech during a reading.

Role-on-the-wall

This strategy has its roots in the character analysis employed by actors to gain greater insights into characters' motivations, but it can be adapted to enable children to explore characters in a text. In order to create a Role-On-The-Wall, children are encouraged to collect information and formulate opinions about a character, with close reference to the text. The activity involves drawing a large outline of the character or characters on a wall or screen. Children discuss and add information about the character to the outline, based on what they know of the text and how they respond to it. The criteria for what is collected and recorded can vary according to the focus of the learning. The information displayed can be added to or changed as children read more of the text, thus supporting discussions on character profiles, character development, relationships with other characters and authorial intent.

Silent movie

This is a light-hearted activity designed to provide a quick overview of a plot or sequence of events. It works best with older children in Years 5-6. Children walk through the events of a whole plot or part of a plot, performing the appropriate actions according to the teacher's narration. They move briskly in a similar manner to a silent movie, but not artificially speeded up. Some children play the characters, whilst others keep up the pace by ushering the actors into the correct scenes at the right times or keep a check on the procedures as the audience. The first run through needs to be a rehearsal, with the second attempt being a performance without any prompts or checks. The Silent Movie strategy is particularly useful with complicated plots, but it can also be used to illustrate sequences in non-fiction texts such as instructions, historical events or sequences in science.

Sound effects

Interrogating the text to identify and create appropriate sound effects for a poem or story help children consider those explicit and implicit auditory aspects of a text that contribute to the meaning. The sounds can be created with instruments, voices and/or objects.

Soundscapes/sound collages/sound machines

This is a more sophisticated version of creating sound effects. It involves the creation of a collage of sounds to paint a picture of the setting, atmosphere or theme of a story or topic and can be combined with dance and movement. Using words from the text, voices and percussion it can also be presented as an imaginary Sound Machine which repeats on a loop until switched off. Key words can be repeated or overlapped to emphasise their significance and increase their impact. The strategy presents an opportunity for children to explore how an author uses words and events to create different moods, atmospheres and suspense.

Spotlighting/overheard conversations

Spotlighting or Overheard Conversations take place whilst groups are improvising spontaneously without an audience. The teacher freezes the action and shines an imaginary spotlight on each group in turn, allowing everyone else to listen in to a snippet of their improvised conversation. Only the group under the spotlight is active. The rest of the class remain silent as an audience.

Spotlighting has the potential to create a deeper understanding of characters and events in texts. Whilst developing speaking and listening through collaborative group work, spotlighting enables all children to perform a short piece of improvisation in whatever way they feel comfortable, with an option to convert their snippets into playscripts or character studies.

Another version of an Overheard Conversation is where the children listen in to the teacher-in-role having an imaginary telephone conversation related to a story. The children listening in have to work out who the character is, where they are, what they are talking about and who they might be talking to. The telephone conversation is conducted by a teacher-in-role in order to present a degree of challenge that encourages further exploration of the story, but older or more confident children can provide similar conversations for others to guess.

Suspense alley

This is presented in a similar way to Conscience Alley, but without a dilemma. Children identify the words and phrases used by an author to create suspense in a particular extract from a novel. The words are shared out amongst the children who stand roughly in the order in which they appear in the text, to form two lines like an alley. A child or teacher-in-role as the main character walks slowly through the alley as the children call out their words to reveal the developing suspense.

Teacher-in-role/adult-in-role

Teacher-in-role, as the term suggests, involves the teacher taking on a role as part of a drama activity. It provides a model of appropriate language and behaviour for role playing and can present alternative perspectives and challenges within the dramatic context. A teacher-in-role can drive a narrative forward, build tension and provide or request key information in response to the particular needs of the children.

It enables a teacher to both challenge and support children from inside the drama, allowing the teacher to co-construct powerful learning environments, where children can gain deeper insights into the meanings of texts (see 'How to manage drama' from the introduction).

Teacher narrator

The teacher acts as a narrator within a drama activity, pausing the process to link key moments, move time on, introduce information, introduce themselves as a teacher-in-role or present a challenge. The narration also models appropriate story language and structure.

Thought tracking

On a signal from the teacher, children in role speak their character's thoughts aloud at a given moment in the drama. Where children are playing themselves within an imaginary situation, their thoughts will represent their own responses to that situation.

Where do you stand now?/the spider's web

Whilst technically not a drama strategy, 'where do you stand now?' is frequently used as part of a drama activity to give children an opportunity to reflect on the issues, characters or events. Each corner or area of the room represents a different opinion. You can place cards at opposite sides of the room saying 'yes' and 'no,' 'agree' and 'disagree' or cards with statements on in different areas. Children choose to stand in the area that best represents their opinions at that moment in time. Those who are undecided must stand either in a central area or closer to one area than another, but need to be prepared to justify their choice. Children move on the word 'Go' and some are then asked to explain their choices. The activity is often repeated to allow children an opportunity to revise their original opinions after listening to the views of others.

In the Spider's Web version, someone stands in the centre of a circle to read out a statement. The person can read out the statement in role or as themselves. On the word '*Go,*' the children in the circle move to stand closer or further away from the person, representing a web of opinions indicating how far they agree or disagree with the statement.

Whole group drama

In whole group drama, both the children and the teacher enter the same imaginary context, moving through the narrative, behaving and reacting as if it were really happening. It is sometimes referred to as 'living through' or 'process drama.' Whole group drama can be paused in order to use other drama strategies to deepen the experience or paused for longer periods to carry out related research or written work. When combined with teacher-in-role, whole group drama is the most effective of all the drama strategies. Through taking part in an imagined experience that feels real, children develop an emotional engagement with the drama. Whole group drama blurs the boundaries between the text and the reader as children share an experience from inside a story.

Basic whole group drama usually has three stages, working in a similar way to a basic story structure:

1   Set up and build belief in the imaginary context.
2   Set a problem or task within the imaginary context and allow the children to respond.
3   Reflect on the experience out of role.

Further reading and resources

Bailey. S. (2021) DRAMA FOR THE INCLUSIVE CLASSROOM. Routledge.
Baldwin. P. (2008) THE PRIMARY DRAMA HANDBOOK. Sage Publications Ltd.
Blank-Kelner. L. (2006) A DRAMATIC APPROACH TO READING COMPREHENSION. Heinemann.
Branscombe. M. (2019) TEACHING THROUGH EMBODIED LEARNING. Routledge.
Branscombe. M. (2021) EMBODIED LEARNING. Minibook Issue 51 UKLA.
Clipson-Boyles. S. (2011) TEACHING PRIMARY ENGLISH THROUGH DRAMA. Routledge.
Cremin. T. et al. (2019) JUMPSTART DRAMA 2nd Edition. Routledge.
Farmer. D. (2011) LEARNING THROUGH DRAMA IN THE PRIMARY YEARS. Drama Resource.
Farmer. D. (2021) DROP OF A HAT DRAMA: Drama Lessons, Games and Activities. Drama Resource.
Grainger. T. (2004) DRAMA, READING and WRITING: Talking Our Way Forwards. UKLA.
Heathcote. D. & Bolton. G. (1995) DRAMA FOR LEARNING. Heinemann.
McDonald. R. (2017) THE REALLY USEFUL DRAMA BOOK. Routledge.
O'Neill. C. (Ed) (2015) DOROTHY HEATHCOTE ON EDUCATION AND DRAMA. Routledge.
Roberts. H. & Kidd. D. (2018) UNCHARTERED TERRITORIES. Independent Thinking Press.
Taylor. T. (2016) A BEGINNERS GUIDE TO MANTLE OF THE EXPERT. Singular Publishing Ltd.
Wagner. B. J. (1990) DOROTHY HEATHCOTE: DRAMA AS A LEARNING MEDIUM. Nelson Thornes.

Current publications by the author

Harrison. L. (2017) RED SNOW. www.troubador.co.uk (Twitter@Larrainesharri3 for signed copies).
Harrison. L. (2020) ANGEL'S CHILD. www.troubador.co.uk (Twitter@Larrainesharri3 for signed copies).

Drama resources

www.artsonthemove.co.uk
www.davidwood.org.uk
www.dramaresource.com
www.intextperformance.com
www.larrainesharrison.com
www.learnerama.co.uk
www.learnthroughdrama.com
www.mantleoftheexpert.com
www.nationaldrama.org.uk
www.playingwithplays.com
www.rsc.org.uk

Other useful links

www.andertontiger.com (Radio for schools)
www.searchingforexcellence.co.uk
www.talkforwritingshop.com
www.ukla.org

Texts

NB: Texts marked * are mentioned in both Parts One and Two.

Part I

Abram. B. (2019) CHARLIE'S BIG IDEA: The Adventures of Grandad Wheels. www.grandadwheels.com.
Ahlberg. J. & Ahlberg. A. (2016) FUNNYBONES. Random House.
Andreae. G. & Wojtowycz. D. (1998) THERE'S A RUMBLE IN THE JUNGLE. Orchard Books.
Armitage. R. & Armitage. D. (2007) THE LIGHTHOUSE KEEPER'S LUNCH. Scholastic.
Berrington. L. (2007) A DAY AT THE SEASIDE: Hattie and Friends. Paw Print Publishing.
Berrington. L. (2019) A DAY AT THE PARK: Hattie and Friends. Paw Print Publishing.
Blackall. S. (2020) IF YOU COME TO EARTH. Chronicle Books.
Brooks. F. (2011) USBORNE ILLUSTRATED BOOK OF NURSERY RHYMES. Usborne.
Browne. E. (1995) HANDA'S SURPRISE. Walker Books.
Bryon. N. (2020) CLEAN UP. Random House.
Campbell. R. (2019) DEAR ZOO. Macmillan.
Carle. E. (2001) THE VERY HUNGRY CATERPILLAR. Hamish Hamilton.
Carle. E. (2019) THE VERY HUNGRY CATERPILLAR'S BIRTHDAY PARTY. Puffin.
Carter. L. (2017) THERE IS NO DRAGON IN THIS STORY. Bloomsbury.
Carter. L. (2021) THERE IS NO BIG BAD WOLF IN THIS STORY. Bloomsbury.
Child. L. (1999) I WANT A PET. Lincoln Children's Books.
Cooper. H. (1998) PUMPKIN SOUP. Random House.
Cooper. H. (2004) A PIPKIN OF PEPPER. Random House.
Cottle. K. (2020) THE BLUE GIANT. Pavilion Children's Books.
Dickins. R. (2007) USBORNE ILLUSTRATED FAIRY TALES. Usborne.
Donaldson. J. (2014) THE GRUFFALO PLAY. Macmillan.
*Donaldson. J. (2014) POEMS TO PERFORM. MacMillan.
Donaldson. J. (2016) THE GRUFFALO. Macmillan.
Donaldson. J. (2016) THE HIGHWAY RAT. Alison Green Books.
Donaldson. J. (2016) ROOM ON THE BROOM. Macmillan.
Doyle. M. (2018) RAMA AND SITA: The Story of Diwali. Bloomsbury.
*Eagleton. I. & Mayhew. J. (2021) NEN AND THE LONELY FISHERMAN. Owlet Press.
Fae. S. & N. G. K. (2019) HARRY SAVES THE OCEAN. N.G.K.
Fielding. R. (2021) TEN MINUTES TO BED LITTLE DRAGON. Random House.
Freedman. C. & Cort. B. (2007) ALIENS LOVE UNDERPANTS. Simon & Schuster.
Ganeri. A. (2008) STORIES FROM FAITHS: Hinduism. Krishna Steals the Butter and Other Stories. Q.E.D. Publishing.
Gliori. D. (2009) NOISY POEMS. Walker Books.
Hart. C. (2016) MEET THE OCEANS. Bloomsbury.
Henn. S. (2021) THE BEST WORST DAY EVER. Simon & Schuster.
Hughes. S. (1993) DOGGER. Red Fox.
Imai. M. (1994) LITTLE LUMPTY. Walker Books.

Jeffers. O. (2005) LOST AND FOUND. Harper Collins.
Jones. G. P. (2021) RABUNZEL. Pea Green Boat Books.
Kinnear. N. (2020) Shhh! QUIET. Alison Green Books.
Lacome. J. (1995) WALKING THROUGH THE JUNGLE. Walker Books.
Ladybird. (2021) LADYBIRD TALES: Classic Collection. Ladybird.
Lonergan. O. (2020) CATS' EYE VIEW OF . . . LITTER. Nielson.
Lumbers. F. (2020) CLEM AND CRAB. Andersen Press.
McKee. D. (1990) ELMER. Andersen Press.
*Mortimer. R. (2020) RED RIDING HOOD AND THE SWEET LITTLE WOLF. Hodder.
Nicoll. H. & Pienkowski. J. (1976) MEG ON THE MOON. Penguin.
Nicoll. H. & Pienkowski. J. (1978) MEG AND MOG. Puffin.
Penfold. A. (2018) ALL ARE WELCOME HERE. Bloomsbury.
Roberts. S. (2019) SOMEBODY SWALLOWED STANLEY. Scholastic.
Rock. L. (2007) LION BIBLE FAVOURITES FOR THE VERY YOUNG. Lion Hudson P.L.C.
Scheffler. A. (2006) MOTHER GOOSE'S NURSERY RHYMES. Macmillan.
Sendak. M. (1992) WHERE THE WILD THINGS ARE. Harper Collins.
Sharratt. N. & Lindsay. E. (2016) SOCKS. Picture Corgi.
Waddell. M. (1995) FARMER DUCK. Walker Books.
Waddell. M. & Bendall-Brunello. J. (1995) THE BIG BAD MOLE'S COMING. Walker Books.
Zetter. N. (2016) ODD SOCKS. Troika Books.
Zucker. J. (2005) LIGHTING THE LAMP: A Diwali Story (Festival Time). Frances Lincoln Publishers.

Part II

Adams. E. (2016) THE GREAT FIRE OF LONDON: Anniversary Edition. Wren & Rook.
Andersen. H. C. (2014) THE LITTLE MERMAID. Hythloday Press.
Anderson. S. (2020) THE CASTLE OF TANGLED MAGIC. Usborne.
Applebaum. K. (2019) THE MIDDLER. Nosy Crow.
Baker. J. (1991) WINDOW. Greenwillow Books.
Becker. H. (2021) COUNTING ON KATHERINE. Macmillan.
Bethell. Z. (2021) THE SHARK CALLER. Usborne.
Bond. M. (2017) PADDINGTON AT LARGE. Harper Collins.
Bradman. T. (2011) PUTTING ON A PLAY: Gunpowder Plot. Hatchett.
Browning. R. (2015) THE PIED PIPER OF HAMELIN illustrated by Kate Greenaway. Create Space.
Browning. R. (2015) THE PIED PIPER OF HAMELIN illustrated by Arthur Rackham. Pook Press.
Bunzl. P. (2016) COGHEART. Usborne Publishing.
Bunzl. P. (2020) SHADOWSEA. Usborne Publishing.
Butler. S. (2018) THE NOTHING TO SEE HERE HOTEL. Simon & Schuster.
Campion. K. (2020) THE LAST POST. Troubador.
Carroll. E. (2017) LETTERS TO THE LIGHTHOUSE. Faber & Faber.
Carroll. E. (2018) SECRETS OF A SUN KING. Faber & Faber.
Carroll. E. (2019) THE SOMERSET TSUNAMI. Faber & Faber.
Carter. J. & Layton. N. (2021) WEIRD WILD AND WONDERFUL. Otter Barry Books.
Chaplin. A. (2012) SAUSAGES FOR TEA. Arts on the Move.
Child. L. (2012) WHO'S AFRAID OF THE BIG BAD BOOK? Orchard Books.
Corbett. P. (Ed) (2002) POETRY ALIVE FOOTPRINTS IN THE BUTTER. Belitha Press Ltd.
Crawford. S. A. (2008) 25 SCIENCE PLAYS FOR BEGINNING READERS. Scholastic.
Cunningham. K. & Cunningham. S. (2016) VLAD AND THE GREAT FIRE OF LONDON. Reading Riddle.
Cunningham. K. & Cunningham. S. (2018) VLAD AND THE FLORENCE NIGHTINGALE ADVENTURE. Reading Riddle.
Dahl. R. (2001) CHARLIE AND THE CHOCOLATE FACTORY. Puffin.
Dahl. R. (2007) JAMES AND THE GIANT PEACH. Puffin.
Dahl. R. (2016) FANTASTIC MR. FOX. Puffin.
Dahl. R. (2016) GEORGE'S MARVELLOUS MEDICINE. Penguin.
Davidson. S. et al. (2019) FORGOTTEN FAIRYTALES OF BRAVE AND BRILLIANT GIRLS. Usborne.

Doherty. B. (1993) STREET CHILD. Harper Collins.
Donaldson. J. (2013) PLAYTIME. Macmillan.
*Donaldson. J. (2014) POEMS TO PERFORM. MacMillan.
Donaldson. J. (2020) BOMBS AND BLACKBERRIES. Hatchett.
Donegan. P. (2018) WRITE YOUR OWN HAIKU For Kids. Tuttle Publishing.
*Eagleton. I. & Mayhew. J. (2021) NEN AND THE LONELY FISHERMAN. Owlet Press.
Farook. N. (2020) THE GIRL WHO STOLE AN ELEPHANT. Nosy Crow.
Farrell. L. (1992) THE TRIAL OF THE BIG BAD WOLF. Mercier Press.
Foreman. M. (1972) DINOSAURS AND ALL THAT RUBBISH. Puffin.
Fransman. K. & Plackett. J. (2020) GENDER SWAPPED FAIRY TALES. Faber and Faber.
French. J. (2019) WHAT A WASTE. DK.
George. R. (1976) ROALD DAHL'S CHARLIE AND THE CHOCOLATE FACTORY: A PLAY. Penguin.
George. R. (2017) JAMES AND THE GIANT PEACH: THE PLAY. Puffin.
Gold. H. (2021) THE LAST BEAR. Harper Collins.
Greaves. S. (2003) COMIC BOOK SHAKESPEARE MACBETH. Timber Frame Productions.
Grill. W. (2014) SHACKLETON'S JOURNEY. Flying Eye Books.
Halligan. K. & Walsh. S. (2018) HERSTORY BOOK. Nosy Crow.
Hardinge. F. (2015) THE LIE TREE. Macmillan.
Hardy Dawson. S. (2017) WHERE ZEBRAS GO. Otter Barry Books.
Hardy Dawson. S. (2020) IF I WERE OTHER THAN MYSELF. Troika Books.
Hardy. V. (2018) BRIGHTSTORM. Scholastic.
Harrison. L. S. (2017) RED SNOW. Troubador.
Harrison. L. S. (2020) ANGEL'S CHILD. Troubador.
Harrison. M. (2021) BY ASH, OAK AND THORN. Chickenhouse.
Hickes. P. (2020) THE HAUNTING OF AVELINE JONES. Usborne.
Howe. C. (2018) LET'S PERFORM. Bloomsbury Ed.
Hughes. T. (2013) THE IRON MAN. Faber & Faber.
Hunt. R. (2011) VIKING ADVENTURES. Oxford Reading Tree.
Jamieson. V. (2017) ROLLER GIRL. Random House.
Kelso. B. P. (2013) PLAYING WITH PLAYS SERIES. Playing with Plays.
Killick. J. (2020) CRATER LAKE. Firefly.
King Smith. D. (2012) THE HODGEHEG. Penguin Modern Classics.
Kirtley. S. (2020) THE WILD WAY HOME. Bloomsbury.
Kuzniar. M. (2020) SHIP OF SHADOWS. Random House.
Lacey. J. (2018) THE DRAGON SITTER'S SURPRISE. Andersen Press.
Lear. E. Illustrated by Beck. I. (2002) THE JUMBLIES. Corgi.
Lynch. P. J. (1995) THE SNOW QUEEN by Hans Christian Andersen. Random House.
Magorian. M. (1983) GOODNIGHT Mister TOM. Puffin.
McCaughrean. G. (2013) THE ORCHARD BOOK OF GREEK MYTHS. Orchard Books.
McGough. R. (2020) CROCODILE TEARS. Otter Barry Books.
McLachlan. J. (2019) LAND OF ROAR. Egmont.
McLachlan. J. (2020) RETURN TO ROAR. Egmont.
McNicoll. E. (2020) A KIND OF SPARK. K.O.
Milway. A. (2019) HOTEL FLAMINGO. Piccadilly.
Montgomery. R. (2020) THE MIDNIGHT GUARDIANS. Walker Books.
Morpurgo. M. (1995) THE WRECK OF THE ZANZIBAR. Heinemann.
Morpurgo. M. (2007) BORN TO RUN. Harper Collins.
Morpurgo. M. (2007) WHY THE WHALES CAME. Egmont.
*Mortimer. R. (2020) RED RIDING HOOD AND THE SWEET LITTLE WOLF. Hodder.
Moses. B. (2009) THE GREAT GALACTIC. Caboodle Books Ltd.
Murray. S. (2020) ORPHANS OF THE TIDE. Puffin.
Noyes. A. (1981) THE HIGHWAYMAN. O.U.P.
Orton. K. (2019) NEVERTELL. Walker Books.
Palmer. T. (2021) ARCTIC STAR. Barrington Stoke.
Parr. L. (2015) THE VALLEY OF LOST SECRETS. Bloomsbury.

Patten. B. (1999) THE PUFFIN BOOK OF UTTERLY BRILLIANT POETRY. Puffin.
Pearce. J. (2019) THE CURSE OF THE MAYA. Loom.
Porter. K. & Wilcox. Z. (2021) FEARLESS: A Graphic Novel. Scholastic Inc.
Pullman. P. (1996) THE FIREWORK MAKER'S DAUGHTER. Corgi Yearling.
Ramirez-Christensen. E. (2021) MY FIRST BOOK OF HAIKU POEMS. Tuttle Publishing.
Rauf. O. Q. (2020) THE NIGHT BUS HERO. Orion.
Reeve. P. (2013) OLIVER AND THE SEAWIGS. Oxford University Press.
Reid. S. (2017) FANTASTIC MR. FOX: The Play. Puffin.
Riley. P. (2016) FORCES AND MAGNETS. Franklin Watts.
Rumble. C. (2020) RIDING A LION. Troika Books.
Rumble. C. (2021) LITTLE LIGHT. Troika Books.
Sacher. L. (2000) HOLES. Bloomsbury.
Said. S. F. (2014) THE OUTLAW VARJAK PAW. Corgi.
Said. S. F. (2014) VARJAK PAW. Corgi.
Sains. C. (2021) THE ALIEN IN THE JAM FACTORY. Walker Books.
Seed. A. (2015) THE SILLY BOOK OF WEIRD AND WACKY WORDS. Bloomsbury.
Seed. A. (2020) INTERVIEW WITH A TIGER: AND OTHER CLAWED BEASTS TOO. Welbeck.
Seed. A. (2021) INTERVIEW WITH A SHARK: AND OTHER OCEAN GIANTS TOO. Welbeck.
Shakespeare. W. (2015) MACBETH. Penguin.
Sherrick. A. (2016) BLACK POWDER. Chickenhouse.
Sherrick. A. (2021) THE QUEEN'S FOOL. Chickenhouse.
Shetterly. M. L. (2021) HIDDEN FIGURES. Harper Collins.
Sorosiak. C. (2019) I COSMO. Nosy Crow.
Sorosiak. C. (2020) MY LIFE AS A CAT. Nosy Crow.
Stevens. R. (2019) I AM A JIGSAW. Bloomsbury.
Stewart. A. (2019) EVEREST. Bloomsbury.
Taylor. T. (2019) MALAMANDER. Walker Books.
Thompson. L. (2020) THE BOY WHO FOOLED THE WORLD. Scholastic.
Tolkien. J. R. R. (2000) THE HOBBIT: illustrated edition. Harper Collins.
Tomlinson. J. (2014) THE OWL WHO WAS AFRAID OF THE DARK. Egmont.
TRUE ADVENTURES SERIES. (n.d.) (Various authors). Pushkin Press.
Tsang. K. & Tsang. K. (2020) DRAGON MOUNTAIN. Simon & Schuster.
Usborne (2003) NIGHT ANIMALS USBORNE BEGINNERS. Usborne.
VOICES SERIES. (n.d.) (Various authors). Scholastic.
Walker. S. M. (2018) EARTH VERSE: Haiku from the Ground Up. Candlewick Press.
Weil. Z. (2019) POLKA DOT POEMS. Troika Books.
Weir. H. (2010) AESOP'S FABLES. Petra Books.
White. E. B. (2014) CHARLOTTE'S WEB. Puffin.
Williams. M. (2006) GREEK MYTHS 1. Walker Books.
Williams. M. (2009) MR. WILLIAM SHAKESPEARE'S PLAYS. Walker Books.
Willis. J. and Korky. P. (2009) THE RASCALLY CAKE. Andersen Press.
Wood. D. (2009) THE BFG: PLAYS FOR CHILDREN. Puffin.
Wood. D. (2009) DANNY CHAMPION OF THE WORLD: PLAYS FOR CHILDREN. Puffin.
Wood. D. (2017) THE TWITS: THE PLAYS. Puffin.
Wood. D. (2017) THE WITCHES: THE PLAYS. Puffin.
Zetter. N. (2017) HERE COME THE SUPERHEROES. Troika Books.

Appendix
Using live radio in schools
By Russell Prue

If you can orchestrate an authentic live radio broadcast with equipment then you can expect a greater level of excitement, engagement, and ultimately better outcomes. I have regularly used technology to increase levels of engagement and attention of the young people that I've worked with. As the educator we can feign ignorance so that learners get on with it themselves. It works well, especially getting pieces of writing read out. There's a greater sense of ownership too, when learners have taken greater control of the activity, they feel much more involved and give so much more. With a live broadcast there's always a deadline and no undo facility. It's real, live and ever so thrilling. Why do this? As well as having something great to share with others at the end by way of a recording, you'll also have created an authentic sense of an audience without putting young people physically in front of that audience. Broadcasting live also gives you the opportunity for live listener comments and feedback and therefore involve more people in the activity.

Reading your piece after hearing your intro-jingle will increase the excitement level by a significant measure. Jingles are short pieces of audio, usually they're just musical but can also be made up of effects 'SFX' and vocal only performances too 'DRY.' They add an amazing feel to the broadcasting experience. You can find lots of these by searching online or make your own using 'Audacity,' a free audio recording program available for Apple® and Microsoft® operating systems.

Scripts are important, the question is whether to have them written on paper or to use tablets or iPads. In 2016/2017, I was broadcasting a series of workshops with a mixed ability Year 5 class over two terms as part as my role as Lead Creative Schools Creative Practitioner. We found there to be a reluctance to redraft and edit using pencil and paper. We wanted to see whether writing our own texts on iPads led to better quality writing. It did and by a noticeable margin. Not only did we get more text, sometimes twice the amount, there was more redrafting and critical editing and that led to better quality scripts.

Buying your own portable or fixed radio studio provides an amazing resource the whole school and community can use for many years. There's a lot you can do for free right now by just using a computer and streaming the audio from its microphone around your network as a live radio feed. Rocket Broadcaster is a free download, it's an APP that runs on your laptop computer and provides a live listening link inside your school. Listening live inside school needs to be arranged at a set time. Many of my School Radio customers broadcast once a week live to all classrooms towards the end of the day on Friday. The 'sense of audience' for

Appendix using live radio in schools by Russell Prue

your young people is real and without any risk or cost as you're only broadcasting inside of the school. You could at least try the concept to see if doing this works for you. You'll always have a recording of the show that you can edit and put up on the school website for parents to enjoy. We haven't talked about music tracks. For purely educational shows you probably don't need to use music unless the show is about music as a subject. However, if you're planning to broadcast shows as part of breaktimes and after school shows, you'll want to have music tracks available to you. Music is very important to young folks; they'll know every word to the latest number one song. If you want to leave in any music tracks that you played in your broadcast, you will have to publish your recording on Mixcloud.com. This is a podcast hosting site that permits the inclusion of musical tracks. It's free although there are some conditions about the number of songs from a single artist permitted in each show. Mixcloud.com have a PRO account that covers the cost of these extra services and it's not expensive. You could use that live streaming service to broadcast your shows to parents. You'd get a live player APP that you put on your school website.

There's so much you can do with a School Radio Station that impacts learning across the whole school. You can reach parents, engage in community activities and generate funding from making and selling adverts in your broadcasts. Parents with businesses are often only too pleased to give a few pounds for a pupil made advertisement on the station. You'll find examples of these on my website together with more ideas and cases studies. It's time to get back to real words and real meanings and embrace language in a new and exciting fashion.

Russell Prue is an author, broadcaster and educator and provides workshops and equipment to schools all over the U.K. as well as regularly hosting educational shows on LearnRadio.Net.

AndertonTiger.com/Russell